Kilcrea Friary
Franciscan Heritage in County Cork

A sketch of Kilcrea bridge, with the friary in the background, by the well-known antiquarian T.J. Westropp. It is dated November 4th, 1890, and is preserved in the Royal Irish Academy, Dublin (Photo: Royal Irish Academy)

Kilcrea Friary

Franciscan Heritage in County Cork

DENISE MAHER

THIS IS THE MILLENNIUM PROJECT OF THE
BRIDE VALLEY COMMUNITY ASSOCIATION

Tower Books
1999

First published in 1999 by
Tower Books
Ballincollig, Co. Cork
in association with the Committee of
the Bride Valley Community Association

ISBN 0-902568-31-0
Typeset by Tower Books; Printed by Shanway Press

This book is dedicated
to the Franciscan friars,
who served God and his
people at Kilcrea friary

Contents

Illustrations

Plates

Preface

The ruins of Kilcrea friary stand as a monument to its glorious past. This was a past full of learning, Christianity and Franciscan life. The friary's architecture is a reminder of a very different time and culture and its history is one of turbulence and sadness resulting in its eventual destruction. With the passing of the centuries its history has begun to fade and consequently there is a risk that this will be completely lost for future generations.

Being mindful of this, the Bride Valley Community Association commissioned this book on Kilcrea friary. It provides an understanding of Medieval Franciscan life and architecture of the time and of how Kilcrea friary formed an important part of this.

As we enter both a new century and a new millennium, the preservation and retention of the history of the friary becomes even more important. It is expected that the next millennium will provide technological advances so great that they cannot even be imagined at present. Hopefully – this publication on Kilcrea friary will remind future generations of the local community of its heritage – full of history, culture, hope and expectations just as it is hoped the new millennium will be. It may serve as a link with the past.

The creation of this publication began as a dream of a group of local people in 1996. Denise Maher of University College Cork's Department of Archaeology was commissioned to do the research work. This involved a detailed review of relevant historical documents, museum research and fieldwork. I wish to thank her and the Archaeology Department for their contribution. Completion of the project would not have been possible without the assistance of Dúchas, FÁS and West Cork LEADER Co-operative Society Ltd., to whom gratitude is expressed. In addition, I wish to thank Pat Daly, Tower Books, for her great contribution.

The completed work represents the fruits of this effort and the realisation of the dream of the members of the Bride Valley Community Association. Without the efforts of its committee this project could not have been completed and the following members deserve recognition for the generous way they gave of their time and commitment: John Purcell, Ann Linehan, Dan

O'Riordan, Eleanor Hosford, Seamus O'Reilly and Carol Trant, as well as past committee members, the local community, businesses and financial institutions.

Is cúis mhór áthais dom mar sin an foilsiúchán seo a chur i láthair an phobail.

> Charles Scanlan,
> *Chairman,*
> *Bride Valley Community Association*

Acknowledgements

The author received a great deal of advice and assistance from various people and institutions in preparing this book for publication. First and foremost she wishes to thank the chairman and members of the Bride Valley Community Association, who commissioned this work and provided constant encouragement. She is also indebted to Ian Dempsey, West Cork LEADER, for his interest and support. She also wishes to thank Professor Peter Woodman and Dr Elizabeth Shee-Twohig, Department of Archaeology, University College, Cork, for facilitating this work, and Angela Desmond, Department of Archaeology, University College, Cork, who administered the project.

The following members of the Franciscan Order courteously dealt with many queries from the author: Fr Ignatius Fennessey, Killiney; Frs Walter Crowley and Angelus Lee, Cork; and Fr Fergal Grannell, Multyfarnham. Mlle Sarah Toulouse, of the Bibliothèque Municipale, Rennes, provided information on the manuscripts in her care; Ms Helen Moloney-Davis, Boole Library, University College, Cork, facilitated many bibliographic enquiries; Fr John Meagher, O.S.A., Fethard, and Mr Paddy Maher, Fethard, assisted with the translation of Medieval Latin sources; Br Colmán Ó Clabaigh, O.S.B., Glenstal Abbey, advised on the Franciscan manuscript tradition; Dr Ann Lynch, Dúchas: The Heritage Service, facilitated many enquiries; Mr Dick Stapleton, Dúchas: The Heritage Service, provided a drawing of the Kilcrea cloister arcade; Dr Neil Buttimer, Cork Historical and Archaeological Society, facilitated the reproduction of illustrations from that society's Journal; Dr Jane Hawkes, Department of Archaeology, University College, Cork advised on art historical aspects of the Kilcrea ivory crucifixion figure, while Mr John Sheehan, Kilmurry, provided historical information on it; Mr Denis Power, Archaeological Survey of Ireland, Dúchas, drew the author's attention to the Kilcrea reliquary; Mr Raghnall Ó Floinn, Antiquities Division, National Museum of Ireland, advised on artefacts from Kilcrea; the Royal Irish Academy, Dublin, and the Royal Society of Antiquaries, Dublin, provided bibliographic assistance and illustrations; Ms Noelle Guinane, Department of Archaeology, University College, Cork printed off numerous drafts of the work; Mr Paul Tassie, Cork, provided many fine photographs of the friary; Mr Tomás Tyner and Mr Charlie Ruxton, Audio-Visual Services, University College, Cork, provided photographic assistance; Ms Rhoda Cronin, Iniscarra, prepared maps and illustrations for the book and, last but not least, Mr Phelim Manning, Kilkenny, prepared the isometric view of the friary.

The compilation of this book would not have been possible without the extraordinary tolerance of the author's husband, John!

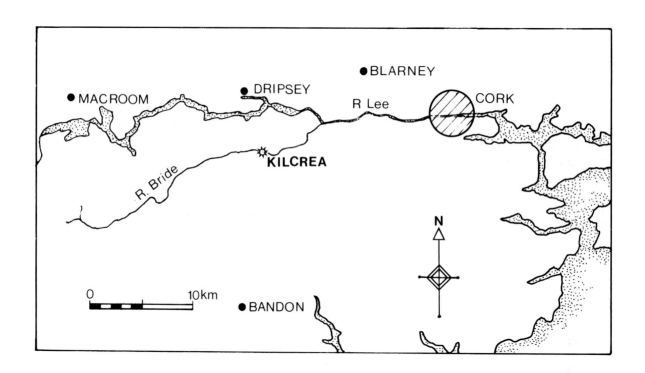

Ill. 2. Map showing the location of Kilcrea (by Rhoda Cronin)

The Franciscans
and Kilcrea

Kilcrea friary is located in the barony of Muskerry, Co. Cork, a short distance west of Cork city (Ill. 2). It was founded in 1465 by Cormac Láidir MacCarthaigh. While 1465 is the generally accepted foundation date, dates of 1470 and 1478 are also on record for the friary. It is strategically located in the rich valley of the Bride River, which runs close by on its north side. The approach to the friary from the northwest is both picturesque and unusual. Travelling over a hump-back bridge, from which a splendid view of the site is to be had, a short walk along a tree-lined grass avenue brings one to the west doorway of the church. In the fields to the west of the friary stand the ruins of Kilcrea castle which was also built by the friary's founder.

The friary was founded for the Franciscan Observants and now stands in ruins. While it has been abandoned for a long time its turbulent history, the impressive survival of its buildings and the stories and legends about those who were associated with it will ensure that it continues to hold an important place in the history of Munster. In order to appreciate its history it is firstly necessary to understand the development of the Franciscan Order, from its origins in Italy to its introduction into Ireland.

St Francis and the Franciscans

Francis Bernardone was born around the year 1182 in Assisi, c.100km north of Rome. He was the son of a rich cloth merchant and, during his youth, he enjoyed a lavish lifestyle. While working for his father he undertook business trips during which he became aware of the development of new types of freelance itinerant preachers throughout Italy. These men sought salvation through voluntary poverty and, unlike most members of traditional monastic Orders, they enthusiastically undertook preaching missions within the rapidly growing towns. These new radicals, embracing poverty and mendicancy, were viewed with some suspicion by the Church. However, they seemed to have made a great impression on Francis who, in spite of his privileged position, appears to have had a genuine sympathy for the poor and the suffering.

In 1205 Francis made the decision to renounce his wealth and lifestyle. He made a complete break with the past and lived as a hermit in various caves and ruinous churches. Within a short

1

space of time he was joined by a few disciples. It is unclear whether Francis was moving towards the lifestyle of a hermit or the more public role of a preacher at this stage. In 1206, however, at Portiuncula, near Assisi, he made his decision. He was attending mass and heard a reading from the Gospel of Matthew in which Christ's instructions to his disciples are given: 'Preach as you go, saying, "The kingdom of heaven is at hand." . . . Take no gold, nor silver, nor copper, nor a staff; for the labourer is worthy of his food'. Henceforward Francis and his followers devoted themselves to preaching, like the other lay freelancers of the time. What differentiated them, however, was Francis' strict rules about poverty. The lifestyle he promoted has been described as a form of organised destitution. He and his followers were wanderers, sleeping in barns and sheds, begging for their daily food and preaching in the streets and market squares. They refused to own property or to touch money.

In effect Francis rejected the values of his own class. In this sense he may be regarded as a rebel who reacted against the co-existence of great wealth and absolute poverty in the booming towns of thirteenth-century Italy. The voluntary poverty which he and his followers espoused identified them with the poor and the deprived. He was joined by followers who were mainly drawn from the aristocracy, the merchant classes and the universities. The preachings of these men, however, had no social or political aims, being mainly focused on the needs for repentance and penance.

By 1210 Francis had twelve followers and together they travelled to Rome to petition Pope Innocent III to approve their rule of life. Innocent had misgivings about them, but he did give verbal approval. Thus the first step in the foundation of the Franciscan Order was taken. Shortly afterwards Francis received Clare of Assisi, a woman from an aristocratic family, into the religious life. This act formed the basis for the establishment of the Franciscan Second Order, known as the Poor Clares. Around the same time a group of lay people asked Francis for his guidance on the secular way of life, and the Franciscan Third Order was formed.

Following the approval of the Order by Pope Innocent the numbers of its followers began to grow rapidly. By 1221 there was no less than 3,000 friars. Official papal approval of the Order was received in 1223. In 1224 Francis received the stigmata. He died in 1226 at Assisi and was canonised two years later.

Even before he died practical problems had surfaced in the running of the Order. The rule which forbade the friars to own property or money made it difficult for the Order to operate effectively. Thus, in 1230, a papal interpretation of this rule was sought from Pope Gregory IX. The result was that the friars were allowed receive gifts of money and property through intermediary trustees. This concession was, in some ways, the beginnings of a withdrawal from Francis' ideal of poverty. Another of his rulings was that there be no distinction of status between ordained and lay members of his Order. Again this gave rise to practical problems; lay friars, for instance, could not dispense the sacraments. In addition, a contemporary Order, the Dominicans, which shared the ideals of the Franciscans, had a competitive edge as it was entirely clerical in composition. In 1239, following internal dissension, a reappraisal of the rule of the Franciscan Order was undertaken and it was decided that lay brothers would be debarred from holding office. Again, one of Francis' basic ideals had been set aside on the grounds of impracticality. The effects of these changes, however, were to allow the Franciscan Order to expand and develop along the lines of other major Medieval religious institutions.

During Francis' lifetime, in 1217, it was decided to begin organised missions from Italy to various countries. Provinces were defined and missionaries were sent to Germany, Hungary, France, Spain, Morocco and the Orient. This universal mission was mainly concentrated on the towns of northern Europe, as only urban centres could support groups of mendicants. Usually the residences of the friars consisted of disused buildings within the city walls. In 1224 it was decided to organise a mission to England and shortly afterwards a party of nine, led by brother Agnellus of Pisa, landed at Dover. The party included Richard Ingworth, an Englishman who joined the Franciscans in Italy. Its first foundation was established at Canterbury, followed by London and Oxford. Over the following five years about twenty Franciscan houses were founded in England.

The Franciscans in Ireland

There is a long tradition of monasticism in Ireland. During the Early Medieval period, which came to an end during the twelfth century, large numbers of monasteries flourished. These were very different in form and organisation, however, from the Later Medieval monasteries. During the twelfth century several major continental monastic Orders were introduced into Ireland, the most important of which were the Augustinians and the Cistercians. After the Anglo-Norman invasion of 1169 the conquerors founded further monasteries for these and other Orders. Thus, by the time of the arrival of the first Franciscans to Ireland, there were several continental Orders established here including the Cistercians, Augustinians, Benedictines, Knight's Templars and Hospitallers.

There is some uncertainty about the date and place of arrival of the first Franciscans to Ireland. Tradition holds that their first friary was founded at Youghal in 1224, followed by Cork in 1229. There is no contemporary historical evidence for this, however, and the roots of the tradition may lie in the possibility that some friars visited these towns in these years simply to assess their potential. It is more likely that the first foundation was in Dublin. Historical sources record that Richard Ingworth, one of the friars who participated in the first Franciscan mission to England in 1224, was given a mission to Ireland in 1231. He became the first provincial of the Order in Ireland and during his term of office friaries were founded at Dublin, Cork, Athlone, Kilkenny, Youghal and, possibly, Cavan and Carrickfergus.

In Ireland, as on the Continent, the Franciscan Order was essentially an urban-based one at this time. It was renowned for its ability to work and interact effectively with the poor and uneducated. This focus on pastoral and community care was the main reason why most Franciscan friaries were founded in urban locations, as it was here that they could have most effect.

The urban locations of most early Franciscan foundations also had political connotations. Some of them were founded under Anglo-Norman patronage and the towns they were located in were colonial. This obviously resulted in an Anglo-Norman/Gaelic-Irish divide within the Order. Twenty-eight of the fifty-eight Franciscan friaries founded before 1508 were under native Irish patronage, and there was Irish involvement in some of the others. Distrust existed between the two groups and during the late thirteenth century Irish-speaking Franciscans were sometimes subjected to close observation by the English authorities. In 1310 it was declared at a parliament held in Kilkenny that those Franciscans who were not of English descent were not to be admitted into 'English' religious houses in Ireland. This rule was, however, repealed shortly afterwards. The invasions by Edward Bruce in 1315 increased the distrust of the English authorities towards Irish friars because of the latters' open support for Bruce. The provincial chapter that met in Dublin in 1324 stated that 'no Irishman could be guardian of one of these houses and all Irish friars, except for some of the most trustworthy, were to be removed from them'. The Statutes of Kilkenny, laid down in 1366, also imposed several restrictions concerning the entry of Irish to religious Orders. For example, it was stated that no religious house in the Anglo-Norman controlled areas of the country should admit Irishmen.

By the early fifteenth century a general decline of standards within the Church, including Orders such as the Franciscans, had set in. However, a second wave of Franciscan activity soon followed. A new movement was introduced from the Continent, the Observant Reform, which sought a more strict observance of the Franciscan rule. It was felt that the Order had moved too far from its original aims. Those Franciscans that did not participate in this reform were called the Conventuals.

Initially these reformers lived individual lives, later coming together to form groups and, ultimately, foundations. The first Irish Observant foundation was established in 1433 at Quin, Co. Clare, and the second was founded at Muckross, Co. Kerry, in 1445. However, these friaries were under the control of the Irish provincial who was normally of Norman descent and consequently was more sympathetic towards the Conventuals. It was Moyne friary, Co. Mayo, which was built sometime before 1456, that became the first true Irish Observant foundation subject to an Observant vicar general. The fifteenth-century period of expansion of the Observants is interesting in that its new foundations were often situated in Gaelic-Irish areas like Connaught and Ulster. The Conventuals, on the other hand, favoured locations within the Pale and in the towns and cities. Part of the reason for the choice of rural locations for the Observants' foundations was their need for solitude to fulfill the aims of the new reform. Therefore, during the fifteenth century, the Irish element within the Franciscans became much stronger and, consequently, the friars become more involved in Gaelic cultural life.

III. 3. Map showing the location and distribution of Franciscan Observant friaries in Ireland *c.*1550 (by Rhoda Cronin after Conlan 1988)

In 1460, Pope Pius II issued a decree appointing Fr Nehemias O'Donoghue as the Irish Observant vicar provincial. Therefore, from 1460 to 1517, the Irish Province was ruled by two provincials – one Observant and one Conventual. This official recognition of the Observants also marked the beginnings of a new period of expansion. Foundations were built in areas where there was an absence of English settlers and older Conventual friaries were sometimes taken over (Ill. 3). By the time of the Reformation the majority of Franciscan houses in Ireland were Observant and there probably was in excess of six hundred friars in the country.

The Reformation

The Protestant reform movements were initiated by the teachings of Luther, Zwingli, Calvin and others. These leaders sought an improvement in the intellectual and moral standards of the Church. They also insisted on the authority of scripture, justification by faith alone and the priesthood of all believers. They rejected the Catholic doctrine of transubstantiation, denying that the bread and wine used in the Eucharist are converted into the body and blood of Christ.

In Germany, Luther's questioning of the authority of the Church led to his excommunication. Nonetheless, his movement spread rapidly, aided by the political, social and economic uncertainties of the age. In England, Henry VIII, despite initially defending the Pope against Luther's teachings, broke with the Catholic Church in 1534 over its refusal to allow him to divorce Catherine of Aragon. He declared himself supreme head of the English Church and began suppressing the monasteries and appropriating Church property. His daughter, Queen Elizabeth, continued his strong anti-Papal stance and became a noted persecutor of Catholics.

The Reformation in Ireland

The first stages of the Reformation in Ireland involved the dissolution of the monasteries, which was legislated for in 1537. Henry VIII's forces suppressed the majority of the monasteries in the anglicised areas of the country. Communities of monks and friars were dispersed and, in some cases, were killed. The *Annals of the Four Masters,* compiled by Brother Micheál Ó Céirigh and three Franciscan colleagues almost a century later, describe the events of the dissolution thus:

Englishmen turned against the Pope . . . they wiped out the Orders to whom worldly possessions are allowed . . . as well as the four mendicant Orders . . . they broke down the monasteries . . . they burned and broke the famous images, shrines and relics of the saints . . . although the persecution of the Roman emperors against the Church was great, it is doubtful if Rome ever produced a persecution as great as this.

By 1547 the majority of Ireland's monasteries had been suppressed and practically all of the remainder were dissolved during the reign of Elizabeth I, 1558-1603.

In some regions outside of the areas of English control the monks and friars were permitted to remain in their monasteries, even after these had been officially suppressed. The Conventual

Franciscans, however, because of the location of their friaries in English-controlled areas, ceased to exist. The Observants were more difficult to suppress and even when their friaries were dissolved they continued working in the neighbourhood and, when the local rulers were sympathetic, they often re-occupied their buildings. Following the accession of Elizabeth 1 to the throne a more systematic period of persecution began. This was partly a side-effect of the rebellions that marked her reign in Ireland. Any religious captured by the English was liable to be put to death and at least thirty-five Irish Franciscan friars were killed during her reign. Others were imprisoned or deported. Most of the remaining friaries ceased functioning and by the end of her reign, in 1603, only five remained in Franciscan hands.

Without friaries it proved difficult to train Franciscan novices. Consequently these were sent to the Continent for their education. Returning to Ireland, these new friars were dedicated to the Counter-Reformation. The first Irish Franciscan continental college, St Anthony's College at Louvain, was founded in 1606, and others were later founded in Rome, Paris and Prague. Without these colleges the Irish Franciscans would probably have become extinct. Between them these colleges trained an average of ten friars each year during the first half of the seventeenth century. The majority of these returned to Ireland where they joined communities which operated in the spirit of the Counter-Reformation. The re-organisation of the Order in Ireland during this period, combined with its strong support system on the Continent, allowed the Franciscans to expand again. This revival, however, ended with the arrival of Cromwell to Ireland in 1649. He attempted to eradicate Catholicism by a reign of terror. Dozens of Franciscans were killed and others were transported to the West Indies. The Order only survived by going underground. By 1660 the situation had improved somewhat, though by this time there were only an estimated two hundred friars left in Ireland.

Following the Battle of the Boyne the period of the Penal Laws began in Ireland. This was to prove devastating for the Franciscans whose overall numbers are estimated to have been reduced from five hundred and nine friars in 1700 to about one hundred and fifty friars in 1782. Many friars obeyed the 1697 Act of Banishment by emigrating and settling in their continental colleges. Others became military and naval chaplains abroad. Those who remained in Ireland lived through sporadic periods of priest-hunting. Some of these registered as diocesan priests, since the Penal Laws were directed more against monks and friars than against the parochial clergy. Frequently Franciscans took charge of parishes close to their old friaries, operating in small well-hidden chapels.

Various political acts improved the position of Catholics in Ireland from the later eighteenth century onwards. These allowed the friars greater freedom and they became more public in their activities. New churches were built by them in the cities, including Dublin, Cork and Limerick. With the establishment of Maynooth College in 1795 more diocesan clergy began to become available. This, in turn, reduced the opportunities for parish work by the friars. Today there are fifteen Franciscan friaries in Ireland.

Kilcrea Friary

The name Kilcrea (Cill Chré) means the Cell of Cere, Cera or Cyra. St Cere, who lived in the sixth century, is said to have founded a nunnery about a mile east of the friary in the parish of St Owen's, now called Ovens. She was the daughter of Dubh, who was of the race of Cornarius and monarch of Ireland, while her mother was from Scotland. According to Smith, the eighteenth-century historian 'Her festivals were celebrated on the 16th of October and the 5th of January, the days of her birth and death respectively'. When the Franciscan friary was founded it became known as 'Kilkere' or 'Kilchre' in her honour. Today its name has been anglicised to Kilcrea. Therefore, it appears that Kilcrea was a location with ecclesiastical associations long before Cormac Láidir MacCarthy founded the Franciscan friary there in 1465. The friary was dedicated to St. Brigid of Kildare.

Cormac Láidir MacCarthy, son of Thady MacCarthy, was Lord of Muskerry (Pl. 3). His nickname, Láidir (strong, great), was appropriate as he was responsible for the building of castles at Kilcrea, Blarney and Dripsey as well as the religious foundations at Kilcrea and Ballyvacadane. He was killed by his brother and nephew at Carrignamuck Castle, Dripsey, in 1494, and is buried in Kilcrea friary.

During the dissolution of the monasteries, which affected county Cork by 1542, Kilcrea remained inhabited by the friars under the protection of the MacCarthys. Neither was their occupation affected during the reigns of Edward VI and Mary. However, Kilcrea was subjected to stern pressure during the reign of Elizabeth.

In 1570 John Perrott became President of Munster and appointed Richard Dixon as Bishop of Cork and Cloyne. He also sent Thomas O' Herlihy, Catholic Bishop of Ross, to London for imprisonment. Here he spent almost four years in the Tower of London before being released due to the efforts of Cormac MacDiarmuid MacCarthy of Muskerry. He died in 1579 and is buried at Kilcrea.

In 1577 the friary and lands of Kilcrea were leased to Cormac Mac Tadhg MacCarthy. It was stipulated by Queen Elizabeth in 1578 that he was not to return the lands to the friars. This was an ironic turn of events as it was his great-grandfather who originally bestowed the lands to the friars. The friars may have evacuated the friary, though if so they did not move too far away.

In 1584, following Cormac MacTadhg's death, the friary was plundered by English soldiers, two of whom died while fighting amongst themselves over the spoils. In 1616-1617 Donatus Mooney wrote an account of this event at Louvain and this is preserved in the Bibliothèque Royale in Brussels (Ms. 3947). The following is a translation of the Latin original:

In the year 1584 some English soldiers passing that area entered the monastery and insolently attacked the images and pictures of the church. Two of them ascended to the place where there was the statue of the Crucifix, with 'tablets' at the four parts of the cross on which were the four evangelists in gold and silver, exquisitely executed not merely by reason of the materials used but especially by the precious artifice of the work itself. When they contested amongst themselves as to which of them could acquire these metals first, and therefore become their property as a spoil, they began to contend with each other and did not desist until they wounded each other. From which wounds, one of them that same night and the other the next night died. All present at this scene meanwhile attributed their case to Divine Justice.

This passage is of interest for a number of reasons, particularly because it mentions some of the furnishings that existed in the friary church at Kilcrea during the later sixteenth century. As well as the metal crucifix, these included 'images and pictures'. Apart from the religious objects dealt with in Appendix 1 and 2, however, no artefacts with Kilcrea associations are known to have survived. There is, however, a nineteenth-century record of the discovery of an 'ancient lead chalice' at the friary.

In 1589, Cormac MacDermot MacCarthy, the nephew of Cormac MacTadhg, was granted the friary. An Elizabethan fiant of 1596 records the leasing of Kilcrea and its lands to Richard Hardinge. In the following year, 1597, one of the most hallowed members of the community died – Thaddeus O'Sullivan. He was buried at night in the cloister outside the chapter-room door.

In 1599 English soldiers were stationed in Kilcrea castle, located nearby, when Cormac MacDermot moved from here to Blarney castle. It was now impossible for the friars to frequent their church as Kilcrea castle directly overlooks the friary. It was probably during this year that the soldiers killed Matthew O'Leyn, an elderly Kilcrea friar.

Catholics were able to repossess their lands and buildings in 1603 under the reign of King James, a Catholic. Shortly afterwards the buildings at Kilcrea were repaired and the friars returned. However, the friary fell into Protestant ownership in 1614, and a record of 1616 states that the friars could no longer live there due to persecution and wars. This record states that there were still four friars living in the vicinity at this time.

The friary was occupied by Cromwellian troops in 1650. In 1661, under the reign of Charles II, it came into the ownership of Donagh, first Lord Clancarty, and remained in this family until the end of the seventeenth century. Some friars continued to hold out in close proximity to the friary. The *Liber Lavaniensis* records the names of all the guardians appointed to the friary from 1629 up until 1717. There are suggestions from local sources that a Friar O'Lonergan served as guardian of Kilcrea from 1782 until 1787, and that the last guardian was a Father E. Hogan who was still alive in 1882. The 1880s marked the end of the Franciscan tradition in Kilcrea and in 1892 it was taken over by the Board of Works as an architectural monument.

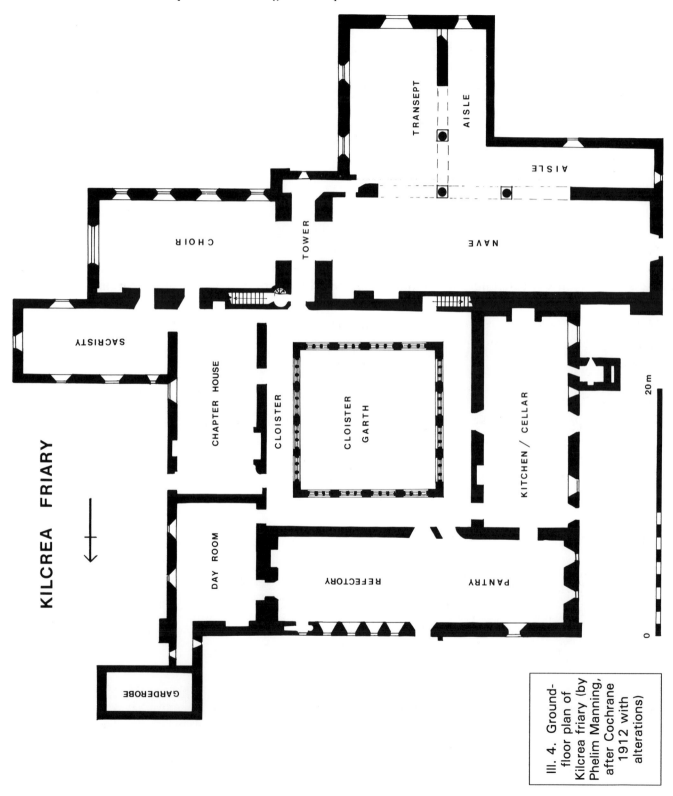

KILCREA FRIARY

Ill. 4. Ground-floor plan of Kilcrea friary (by Phelim Manning, after Cochrane 1912 with alterations)

TRANSEPT

AISLE

AISLE

CHOIR

TOWER

NAVE

SACRISTY

CHAPTER HOUSE

CLOISTER

CLOISTER GARTH

KITCHEN / CELLAR

DAY ROOM

REFECTORY

PANTRY

GARDEROBE

0   20 m

The Architecture
of Kilcrea

Franciscan friaries of the fifteenth and sixteenth centuries differ from those of the thirteenth century in terms of situation. Generally they are found in rural rather than in urban locations. There is also a difference in the architectural layout, with the claustral buildings being generally located south of the church in the earlier period and north of it in the later. Kilcrea was an ideal location for the building of a friary due to its close proximity to a water source and good arable land. In its overall plan the friary follows the general layout of the Irish Franciscan establishments of the period, which incorporates a church and the usual domestic ranges located round a cloister to the north (Ill. 4). There are some additions in Kilcrea, however, which will be referred to below.

In general the architecture of Kilcrea is plain and most of the windows consist of oblong opes or plain pointed lights. Perhaps the most striking architectural feature in the friary is the arcades of the church's nave and transept, despite the simplicity of their design. They contrast strongly with the solid simplicity of the opposing wall and serve to increase the sense of spaciousness within the church. Overall the friary is carefully laid out on a square.

The Church

The church is entered through a doorway situated in its west gable. It consists of a nave and chancel divided by a tall, slender tower. The nave was the part of the church in which the congregation was accommodated. It was made larger by including a south aisle, a transept with two chapels and a transept aisle. The interior of the church, as well as the rest of the friary buildings, has functioned as a graveyard since the seventeenth century and consequently it features a large number of burial monuments.

The nave measures 25.95m in length by 7.20m in width and is entered through a doorway which measures 2.40m in height by 1.49m in width. It consists of a plain pointed arch with broad chamfering. The original door was designed to be closed using a large timber drawbar, the sockets for which survive on the inside. A recess for a holy water stoup is located outside the doorway to the right. Situated in the gable over the doorway are the remains of a large,

11

three-light traceried window. Only the heads and parts of the jambs survive (Pl. 4). Its position is such that in the evenings it would have allowed the nave to bathe in light.

Elsewhere the nave is lit by three windows. The first consists of a deeply recessed pointed example set in the angle between the tower and the nave. The other two occur towards the east end of the north wall, overlooking the cloister. Both of these feature two lights but only the eastern one survives intact. Beneath these windows is a pair of plain, arched tomb-recesses. The eastern one has been widened to hold a Medieval grave-slab (Ill. 14). Tomb recesses such as these were reserved for the burial of important people. Directly opposite them is the tomb of Art O'Leary, enclosed by wrought iron railings. A small, pointed holy-water stoup is situated at the west end of the nave's south wall.

An arcade separates the nave from the south aisle and transept (Pls. 5, 6). This consists of three pointed, broadly-chamfered arches which spring from the side-walls and rest on circular plain-moulded pillars. An arcade of two similar arches separates the transept from its aisle. A skew-arch originally sprung from the angle of the aisle to the junction of the two arcades. However, only its springing-blocks survive.

The south aisle measures 13.80m in length by 3.20m in width. It is entered from the nave through the arcade and is lit by two windows. One of these is in the south wall and consists of the remains of the lower part of a splayed window; the other occurs in the west wall and consists of a tall, narrow, single-light with its head missing. Much of the western half of this aisle is occupied by a large tomb.

The transept measures 12.65m in length by 7.20m in width. It is lit by three windows. The largest and most impressive of these is in the south gable and consists of a four-light example. Its tracery is completely missing, though in design this probably resembled the east and west windows of the chancel and nave respectively. The east wall features two round-headed windows, each of which is flanked by a piscina on its south. A piscina is a stone basin provided with a drain and is usually set in a small wall-niche. It was used for washing the sacred vessels. The location of two piscinae here suggests the former presence of two side-altars in the transept. These altars were normally used for saying masses for the souls of the friary's benefactors.

The transept aisle measures 12.65m in length by 3.10m in width. It is entered from the nave through the arcade. It is lit by a two-light ogee-headed window with an angular hood-moulding on the outside. At the end of the aisle access was gained to the transept through a simple, pointed doorway.

The church tower is of typical Franciscan type – tall and slender. It rests on four large piers each of which is chamfered at the angles. The tower separates the nave from the chancel of the church and is pierced by two large round-headed arches. A low lintelled passageway, which measures 3m in length and .95m in width, leads into the transept from the southwest corner of the base of the tower.

Pl. 1. A detail of Giotto's *The Funeral of St. Francis.* This famous fresco was painted in the Bardi Chapel, Church of Santa Croce, Florence, in 1318 (Photo: John Sheehan)

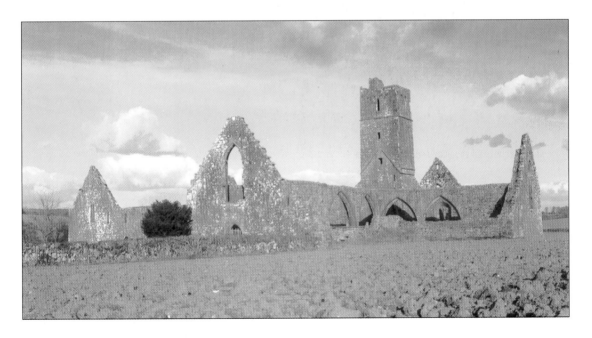

Pl. 2. A general view of Kilcrea friary from the south-west. Observant friaries like this were normally built in rural locations (Photo: Paul Tassie)

Pl. 3. A carved human head which is located high up on the north-east corner of Kilcrea castle. This castle was built by Cormac Láidir MacCarthy, the founder of the friary, and local tradition holds that this is a representation of him.

(Photo: Paul Tassie)

Pl. 4. The west gable of the church with the remains of its large three-light traceried window.
(Photo: Paul Tassie)

Pl. 5. A view, from the west door-way, of the nave of the church. On the right is the arcade which separates the nave from the aisle and the transept. The nave is separated from the chancel by a tower which is typical of Franciscan friaries – tall and slender.
(Photo: Paul Tassie)

Pl. 6. A view, from the transept of the arcades which separate it from the nave and the aisle. These form the friary's most striking feature and increase the sense of spaciousness within the church. (Photo: Paul Tassie)

Pl. 7. This two-light window with its external hood-moulding is located in the south wall of the sacristy.
(Photo: Paul Tassie)

Ill. 5. The chancel's east window, shown here in its reconstructed form, was an impressive, four-light, traceried example. This was the largest and most accomplished window in the friary (after Cochrane 1912)

The tower contained four storeys each of which had a timber floor supported on stone corbels. These storeys were lit by plain, narrow, flat-headed windows, except for the uppermost one where there is a single ogee-headed light in each wall. There are no large windows in the tower. An arched doorway, situated at the north-east angle of the tower, gives access to its stairway. This rises in both straight and spiral sections before finally ascending as a spiral to the top of the tower. There are sixty-three steps in total. The battlements have fallen from their position on top of the tower. Towers in Medieval friaries primarily functioned as belfries. However, the floors within them could also be used for accommodation. There are also some recorded instances of side towers being used for refuge in times of danger.

The chancel of the church measures 14.75m in length by 7.10m in width. It is lit by what originally was an impressive four-light traceried window located in its east gable (Ill. 5). The tracery and mullions are now missing, with only the sill, head and jambs surviving. The south wall features four windows. Three appear to have consisted of double-pointed lights while the easternmost one, which survives intact, consists of a wide, single-light with a pointed arch. Together these five windows insured that the chancel was the brightest part of the church.

No trace survives of the high altar which would have been positioned beneath the east window. An arched piscina, however, occurs nearby in the south wall. Rows of wooden choir stalls would have stood in the chancel positioned parallel with its side-walls. Originally an arched doorway connected the chancel with the east range of the domestic buildings. When the adjoining sacristy was built, however, this was blocked up and replaced by a doorway leading into the sacristy. Traces of the original doorway may still be seen, partly obscured by a tomb.

Beneath the piscina a modern plaque marks the grave of Bishop Thomas O'Herlihy while opposite it another, located in a tomb niche, marks that of Cormac Láidir MacCarthy (see chapter on Burial Monuments).

Sacristy and Scriptorium

The gable-ended building which is located in the angle between the east range and the chancel is clearly a later addition to the main friary. Based on the form of its first floor windows it is likely to be sixteenth century in date. Measuring 12.20m in length and 4.85m in width it comprises two floors, both entered from the corresponding levels of the adjoining east range. The ground floor, which is also connected to the church's chancel by a doorway, would have functioned as a sacristy. The upper floor was almost certainly the monastic scriptorium.

The sacristy was a necessary adjunct to the chancel. Here the sacred vessels, vestments and books which were used for services in the church were kept, and the room was probably furnished with wooden cupboards. It is lit by four windows. The one in the south wall consists of a two-light pointed example fitted with an external hood-moulding (Pl. 7). The two in the north wall are of double ogee-headed type while the eastern example is a pointed two-light window similar to that in the south wall.

The first floor of this building has been identified as Kilcrea's scriptorium. It is the best lit room in the friary, containing no less than eleven windows (ten of which are of double-light type). Both flat- and round-headed types occur. It is because of this profusion of windows that this room has been identified as the Medieval scriptorium, as the scribes would have needed as much light as possible to carry out their work. Originally this room featured a tall window in the east gable, but this was later blocked up and a fireplace inserted in its place. It is likely that this was done due to the necessity of keeping the scriptorium warm and free from dampness.

The Cloister

The cloister usually consisted of a square garth or garden surrounded by covered walkways (ambulatories) on each of its four sides. The cloister was the inner sanctum of a monastery, the centre of all monastic life, and served many functions. The covered walkways, into which sunlight shone through the arcade, provided easy access to the church and domestic buildings on all sides and to the stairways serving the dormitories above. They also could afford peace and

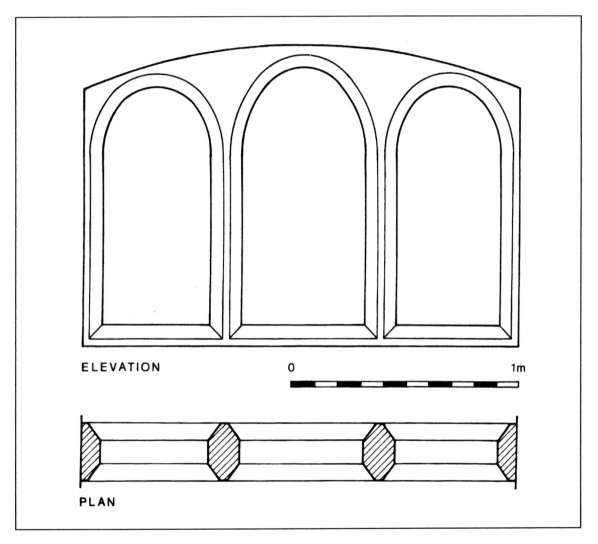

ELEVATION   0   1m

PLAN

Ill. 6. This drawing shows, in reconstructed form, how one of the bays of the Kilcrea cloister arcade would have looked. The arcade no longer survives but architectural fragments from it have recently been discovered. An impression of the overall form of the cloister may be gained from Ill. 7 (by Phelim Manning based on a survey by Dúchas: The Heritage Service).

quiet which was essential for reading and meditation. The monks would spend a good deal of their allotted periods of prayer and meditation here. The garth area in the centre of the cloister may have accommodated a lawn, but it seems more likely that it functioned as a vegetable or herb garden.

The cloister at Kilcrea is square in plan, measuring 17.3m. The church lies to its south and its east, west and north sides are flanked by two-storeyed ranges of buildings. The walkways along its sides do not survive, though the corbels and string-coursing on the walls above indicate the position of the sloping roof which covered them. In a recent FÁS clean-up scheme at the friary a number of lost cloister-arcade fragments were recovered at the friary. Originally these would have formed the arcade which framed the cloister garth (see Ills.6 and 7 for reconstruction).

The cloister is entered from the ground-floor area of the tower through a chamfered, pointed-arched doorway. Access to and from the surrounding ranges is through a number of similar doorways. Three of these occur in the east wall, one in the north wall and one in the west wall.

Domestic Buildings

Normally the east range of buildings in a Franciscan friary contained the sacristy, chapter room and the day room, with the dormitory occupying its first floor level. A garderobe was sometimes located at its northern end, serving the dormitory above. The east range was usually the first of the domestic ranges to be built, featuring, as it did, some of the more important monastic rooms. The chapter-house was the location of daily meetings. Here the monks would gather each morning after mass to hear a chapter of the Franciscan Rule being read and to receive their daily duties and instructions from the friary's superior. In addition, any other business of the friary was discussed here.

Kilcrea adheres fairly closely to the basic Franciscan plan in the layout of its domestic ranges. Its east range measures 24.75m in length by 6.37m in width. The ground floor, from south to north, features a chapter room and a day room separated by the remains of an inserted dividing wall. The day room probably functioned as a place where the friars carried out work during inclement weather. Originally the west range also included a sacristy at its southern end, but this was relocated in the sixteenth century. The entire length of the upper floor functioned as a dormitory.

There are several doorways located in the ground-floor level of the east range. Three occur in the west wall, one of which is blocked, and these provided access to the cloister. There is also a poorly preserved fourth doorway at the south end of this wall, which may be original. Opposite it is a segmental-arched doorway which leads from the chapter room into the later sacristy. The construction of this presumably dates to the same period as the building of the sacristy. Beside it, in the south wall, is the original sacristy doorway, now blocked up. Midway along the east wall is another doorway, now blocked up, which led to the area outside the friary where the cemetery may have been located. This floor also features two large inserted fireplaces: one in the north wall, which partly blocks a window to its west, and one midway along the west wall. The ground floor is lit by four windows each of which is located in the east wall. They are all blocked up. A round-arched recess, which was later converted into a doorway, occurs at the north end of the west wall. It too is now blocked up. Another recess occurs in the south wall and a small wall cupboard occurs in the east wall.

The upper floor of the east range served as a dormitory. It was accessed through a doorway in its south gable which is located at the top of a straight flight of stairs, ascending from the base of the tower. These were the 'night stairs' which the friars would descend on their way to nocturnes, affording direct access from the dormitory to the church. A small slit opening at the landing on top of the stairs provided a view of the chancel. Perhaps this was used by aged or infirm monks who could not attend night prayers. Close to this doorway, in the east wall, is an inserted pointed arched doorway which gives access to the scriptorium. The floor of the dormitory was of timber planking supported on large, transversely-disposed wooden beams. The beam holes of these survive along both sides of the range. This floor is lit by sixteen flat-headed windows and by a large, two-light, ogee-headed example in the north gable.

From the dormitory access is gained through a pointed doorway in the north gable to a passage which led to the garderobe (a medieval latrine). This *domus necessarium* is located in a later gabled building which may have replaced an earlier garderobe. The garderobe was serviced by a chute which debouched at the base of the east wall.

The ground floor of the north range measures 23.40m in length by 6.45m in width. Access is from the cloister through a pointed-arched doorway situated towards the west end of the south wall. Another doorway, now blocked up, occurs immediately opposite this in the north wall. There is slight evidence for an external porch to this doorway. The two doorways may have originally been linked by a passageway, dividing this range into two rooms. The eastern one was more than likely the refectory, based on its large windows. The western end, which contains the large nineteenth-century mausoleum of the Hayes family, probably served as the pantry. The refectory is lit by five, large, pointed windows located in the north wall. More than likely a reader's desk stood in the easternmost window. The curved back of the reader's seat still remains in its west jamb. During the friars' meals passages of scripture or homilies would have been read aloud to them from this position. A large recess occurs nearby in the east wall.

The room presumed to have been a pantry was originally connected by a doorway to the kitchens in the adjoining west range. This is now blocked up and is partly obscured by the Hayes' mausoleum. The room was lit by four windows, one of which was in the west gable. All are now blocked up.

The upper floor of the north range probably also functioned as a dormitory. It was accessed from the dormitory in the east range through a large doorway while a smaller doorway, now

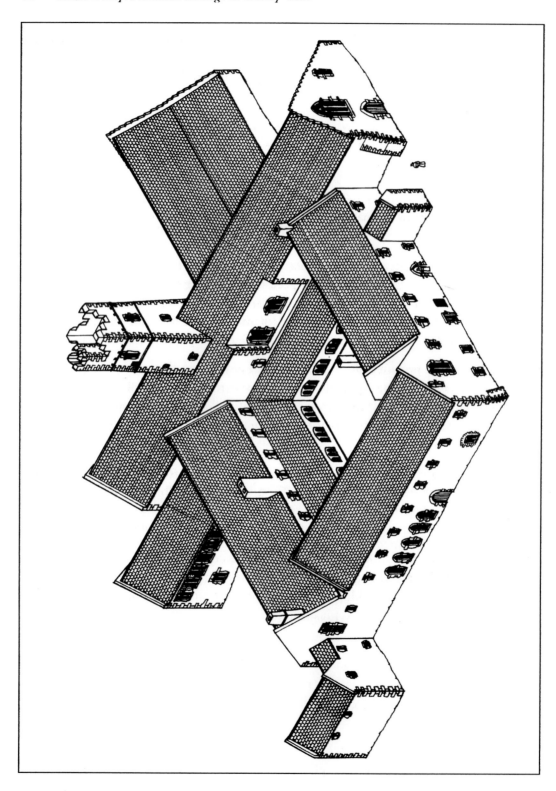

Ill. 7. An isometric reconstruction of Kilcrea friary, from the north-west, showing how it may have appeared in the sixteenth century (by Phelim Manning)

blocked up, leads from it to the upper floor of the west range. This dormitory was lit by sixteen windows, most of which are identical to those in the east range dormitory. A particularly fine two-light window occurs in the east gable. Like the east range dormitory this room was floored on large timber beams.

The west range measures 17.10m in length by 6.45m in width. Access from the cloister is through a pointed-arched doorway which is situated midway along its east wall. A second blocked-up doorway is discernible a short distance to the north of this. Directly opposite the first doorway is another, now blocked up. A flat-headed doorway, situated in the west wall, provides access to a small, two-storeyed, gable-ended structure which is a later addition. Its tiny ground floor apartment is lit by a small looped window which is furnished with a slop-stone underneath. A small wall cupboard also occurs in this room.

Two fireplaces occur in the ground floor of the west range, one in the south gable and one towards the north end of the east side-wall. The latter appears to have been an original feature. This floor was lit by four windows, two of which have double-lights, one of which is now blocked up. Because of the existence of the fireplaces and its location adjacent to the pantry and refectory it is thought that this room functioned as the friary's kitchen.

The first floor of this range probably also functioned as a dormitory. Access is by means of the aforementioned doorway from the upper floor of the north range as well as by a stairway which ascends from the south side of the cloister. Like the similar stairway in the east range this functioned as a 'night stairs'. A narrow slit-opening near the top of the stairs allows a view of the side altars in the south transept.

This dormitory, like the others, was floored on large timber beams and was lit by eleven windows, one of which is ogee-headed. A fireplace also occurs on this floor in the centre of the south gable. It features a joggled arch and rests on two corbels. A small garderobe, accessible from the dormitory, is located within the upper storey of the adjoining gabled building.

In general terms the architecture of Kilcrea friary may be described as functional. Nevertheless, the planning of its layout was sophisticated and demonstrates admirable logic and formality. The good state of preservation of the buildings makes the task of reconstructing daily life in the friary in the mind's eye both feasible and pleasing.

Ill. 8. An illustration from *Les Moines De Kilcré*, a long poem based on monastic life in Kilcrea. The French translation of the original, by Le Chevalier de Chatelain, was published in London in 1858

Franciscan Writings and
the Rennes Manuscript

Scriptoria and Libraries

A scriptorium is a room set apart for writing, especially in a monastic context where it was usually located above the chapter room. It served as the monastic library and was also the place where friars worked as scribes, illuminators and bookbinders. The hours were long and each daylight hour was a working one, except those devoted to liturgical duties. The short and cold days of winter were not favourable times for scribes to work, and completion of texts was often postponed until the summer months. The strict observance of silence was a rule of the scriptorium. Communication with other scribes was by means of notes written along the margins of the texts. Such notes (colophons) still survive on some manuscripts.

Scriptoria were used by certain resident friars, lay-brothers, secular scribes and friars from other Franciscan establishments. In the cases of non-resident scribes, board and lodging would be provided with the friary acting as patron to these scholars. There are also recorded cases of secular scribes later being accepted into the community as friars. The traditional book-hand was the style of script that pervaded in the monastic scriptoria, rather than the less formal and more cursive styles of writing work-shops set up in towns. Among the materials required by the scribe were ink, an inkhorn, a brush, a pen-knife and a bowl for pigment.

While no complete list exists of those Irish Franciscan friaries which had scriptoria and libraries, in some cases it is possible to suggest which ones had. This is based on the presence or absence of a well-lit room in such buildings. For example, it is likely that Kilconnell, Kilcrea, Timoleague, Multyfarnham and Sherkin were amongst those friaries which had scriptoria as each of these feature rooms with multiple windows.

At Kilcrea the scriptorium forms, perhaps, one of the more interesting aspects of the friary. It is located above the sacristy, immediately north of the chancel. Its most striking aspects are the multitude of windows in it and its fireplace (Pl. 9). Both light and heat were essential in order for a scribe to endure painstaking hours of writing while ventilation and heat combined to reduce the possibility of dampness. One would expect the scriptorium of Kilcrea to have been a productive one. To date, however, the only known surviving evidence is a manuscript which is preserved at the Municipal library at Rennes, France where it is registered as Ms. 598.

The Franciscan friars had a reputation of being great book collectors. Across Europe they kept the most flourishing libraries. By the fourteenth century the friary of Sacro Convento at Assisi, for example, had the largest collection of books in the world after the Sorbonne and the Pontifical Library at Avignon. Information about the Irish Franciscan libraries rarely survives, however. Some of the better known early examples were located in the friaries at Donegal, Ennis, Youghal and Timoleague. There is no doubt, however, that the majority of monasteries were equipped with at least a small library. It must also be borne in mind that many libraries were destroyed, or their holdings were scattered, during the various periods of turmoil and upheaval in the middle ages. The dissolution of the monasteries in the sixteenth century resulted in the destruction of several important Franciscan libraries. Some books did escape this fate, however, as a result of being hidden or entrusted to the care of friends, and some were sent to the Continent for safe-keeping.

The only known catalogue of a pre-Reformation Irish Franciscan library's holdings is that of Youghal, which was compiled at different stages between 1490 and 1523. In 1490 the total number of volumes amounted to 140, and by 1523 it was 169. The majority of the books, which were mostly hand-written, may be categorised under the headings of theology, philosophy, Church history and scripture. This catalogue is now preserved in the Berlin Library. During the seventeenth century a number of Irish manuscripts were sent to the Continent for safe-keeping. Some of these were returned to Ireland during the nineteenth century and are now housed in the Franciscan Library, Killiney. Others, however, remained in continental libraries, such as that in St Isidore's College, Rome.

Franciscan Writings

The writings of the Irish Franciscans during the Post-Medieval period may be generally classed as historical, devotional and pastoral. The first type was motivated, perhaps, by a perceived need to re-assert Ireland's claim to be the Island of Saints and Scholars and to encourage pride in the Irish Catholic past. This is especially the case in the writings of the seventeenth century, a period when the reformed religion was in force and the Catholic one was under threat. The devotional writings and pastoralia, on the other hand, comprise sermons, prayer books, hymns, catechisms and collections of edifying stories − known as exempla − which were brought together to help preachers. Works of travel literature and topography were also produced, and in certain cases these may be classed as devotional or ecclesiastical topography. It must be stated, however, that classifying Franciscan writings as historical or devotional is not always a straightforward exercise as the original writer may have, for instance, intended an apparently historical work to be devotional.

Irish Franciscans were prolific in their literary output over the centuries, both at home and abroad. There were three main periods of production: the thirteenth century (Anglo-Norman Period); the fourteenth and fifteenth centuries (Irish Resurgence Period) and the seventeenth century (Counter Reformation Period). The importance of preaching for the Irish Franciscans is evident, especially in the latter half of the thirteenth century, by the extensive amount of *exempla* literature on record. The *exempla,* collections of edifying stories, were compiled by a number of Franciscans from a variety of sources and were regarded as important aids for preachers in their efforts to explain particular morals and Christian virtues. The stories of the *exempla* were told in order to capture and hold the attention of listeners. In the 1250s, Fr Deodatus, provincial at the time compiled such a work. His *Exempla Deodati* was later quoted from in *Liber Exemplorum,* an important and popular work which was written around 1275 by a Friar Minor. The unnamed-author was an Englishman who was educated in Paris and spent most of his years in Ireland. He states in this work that he was lector in Cork around 1267. The book, which comprises over two hundred chapters, drew on a wide range of sources including the Bible, the lives of the saints and experiences (both personal and of others) from both Ireland and abroad. Written in Latin, it was an international work. Only one manuscript copy of it survives, though some material contained in it is also found in a fifteenth-century manuscript in Balliol College, Oxford.

Other Franciscan writings include a book of sermons by Fr de Wycumbe, from which one *exemplum* was quoted. A Fr Thomas of Ireland also produced a book for preachers, *Promptuarium Morale Sacrae Scripturae*. This was compiled by amalgamating various scriptural texts appropriate to the different feast-days. It also gives notes on the lives of the saints and was edited in Rome in 1624 by Fr Luke Wadding. In the 1280s Fr Malachy of Limerick wrote a book on the seven deadly sins – *Venenum Malachie*. This work consists of sixteen chapters of treatises on Christian virtues and includes some *exempla*. In this work Malachy condemns immoral customs of the women of the time. He refers to the Irish as being of Greek origin and, while he acknowledges that the island remains free of poisonous reptiles, he noted that 'the poison remains here in the hearts of men'. It was an important aid for preachers and enjoyed wide circulation in Europe during the middle ages. An edition of it was printed in Paris in 1518. There are at least thirty-six surviving manuscript copies of this work.

By the early fourteenth century a crisis had developed within the English lordships of Ireland as a result of political and economic events. The revival of the Gaelic language and culture was an inevitable consequence. It was also during this century that the Franciscans began to become more integrated with the native Irish. In the fifteenth century new friaries were founded in rural areas rather than in towns. This was especially the case in the south and south-west of Ireland where the population remained essentially native. Gaelicisation, combined with their new Observantine movement, characterised the Franciscans of the fifteenth century.

By at least the end of the fourteenth century the friars had begun to write in Irish. Among these works are sacred poems by the Westmeath friar Tadhg Camchosach Ó Dalaigh (late fourteenth century) who composed *Peregrinare Pro Christo*. Other poets include Philip Ó hUiginn, whose *Tuar Feirge Foighde Dé* was the first piece printed in the Irish language. Ó hUiginn's other works included poems on St Francis, St Dominic, the Crucifixion, the Blessed Virgin, death and God's mercy. This Gaelic phase also saw the composition of Irish texts, for example TCD Ms. F 5 3. This contains the Latin originals of some well-known Irish texts, both romantic and devotional, and also features tracts on confession. It is now preserved in Trinity College Dublin and was probably written in a Franciscan house in Clare. The manuscript preserved in Rennes, France, which is associated with Kilcrea friary, contains several tracts on poverty, Irish translations of patristic texts, sermons and homilies. It also includes an Irish translation of the Travels of Sir John Mandeville. This manuscript will be considered in more detail below.

The third phase of Irish Franciscan writings occurred in the seventeenth century. It was during this century that Irish scholarship was at its zenith, both in national and international terms, and the Irish Franciscan movement played a major role in this. Perhaps the two most important centres which contributed to this great literary output were St Anthony's at Louvain and St Isidore's at Rome. Both of these Franciscan colleges were founded in the early seventeenth century for Irish students. At this time the doctrines of the Reformation were being rigidly enforced in Ireland and it was impossible for a Catholic to produce any religious book which would be seen as being against these new doctrines. St Anthony's College was founded as a result of several pleas made by the Irish Franciscans. After the destruction of the Donegal friary in 1601, the Franciscans needed a safe college on the Continent for their students and novices. In 1607 Pope Paul V gave papal sanction for the college and its first superior was Fr Donagh Mooney. Louvain was to become one of the most important Irish centres for learning on the Continent. In 1611 Fr Bonaventure O'Hussey printed the first catechism in the Irish language – T*eagasg Críosaidhe* – at Antwerp. It was reprinted at St Anthony's, Louvain and again in Rome in 1707. O'Hussey was also the author of several devotional poems and produced the first Irish grammar – *Rudimento Grammaticae Hibernicae*. In 1616 Florence Conry published an Irish translation of the Spanish devotional work *El Desseoso,* and in 1619 Fr Hugh MacCaughwell published the *Statan Sacramuinte na hAitride*. Both of these writers were to prove dynamic figures in the development of the intellectual life of St Anthony's College. Also amongst the Irish literati at this time was Fr Luke Wadding, who was associated with St Isidore's from its foundation in Rome in 1625 to his death in 1657. He spent much of this time working on a comprehensive history of the Franciscans, and this resulted in some of his more famous works: the eight folio volumes of the *Annales Minorum* (Lyon, 1625-1657), the *Scriptores Ordinis Minorum* (Rome, 1650) and sixteen folio volumes on the writings of Johannes Scotus, the Medieval philosopher (Lyon, 1639). Other famous seventeenth-century Franciscan works include *Acta Sanctorum Hiberniae* and *Triadis Thaumaturgae,* published by Fr John Colgan in 1645 and 1647 respectively.

The single most important Franciscan work of the Post-Medieval Period was the compilation of Irish history popularly known as the *Annals of the Four Masters.* This great compilation was produced in a temporary shelter at Bundrowes, near the Franciscan friary of Donegal, between 1632 and 1636. The four friars it is named after were Micheál Ó Clérigh, Fearfeasa Ó Maolchonaire, Cúchoigcríche Ó Duibhgheannain and Cúchoigcríche Ó Cléirigh. It consists of a historical mosaic of Ireland's history put together by collecting the information in manuscripts such as the *Annals of Ulster*, the Clonmacnoise original of the *Chronicon Scotorum*, the *Annals of Tigernach* and other sources. Although it was intended by Ó Cléirigh that it be published through the Irish printing-press at Louvain, unfortunately, however, this famous school could not afford to do so and it was not published until 1851.

Both St Isidore's and St Anthony's were extremely important in the role they played in preserving and enriching Irish religion, history, learning and literature. The themes incorporated in the Franciscan writings of the Medieval period are vast. They include devotional and historical writings as well as travel log literature. They embrace not only Franciscan spirituality but also aspects of the Gaelic Resurgence and other contemporary political and social movements. The period from the fourteenth to the sixteenth centuries saw a relocation of the manuscript tradition to the west and south of Ireland, involving both native Irish and Gaelic-Norman families. Study of such works is crucial in order to gain an insight into the mechanisms employed by the Franciscans in their roles as religious instructors, Counter Reformationists and historical chroniclers.

THE RENNES MANUSCRIPT

This manuscript, which was written in Ireland, remained there until the seventeenth century. During the eighteenth century it came into the ownership of Président Christophe-Paule de Robien (1698-1756), a well-known collector, lawyer and antiquarian. Later on in the century it became the property of the municipal library of Rennes, Brittany, as a result of the confiscations that followed the French Revolution. A colophon (marginal note) on f. 69 clearly indicates its association with Kilcrea friary.

The manuscript measures 27cm in height and 20cm in width and consists of about 125 folios of poor quality parchment. The text, which is laid out in two columns, is in semi-uncial script and is written in a brownish-black ink (Pl. 10). The language used is predominantly Irish, though there are a few words in Latin. There are a number of illuminated initial letters painted either in red, ochre and black or red and green, while others just have a touch of colour rather than being fully illuminated. A selection of the initials are zoomorphic in style, for example those on folios 6 and 9, while others are anthropomorphic, for example those on folios 6 and 48. There is a drawing of a hand on the margin of folio 4 which 'points' towards a specific passage. The decorative initials are of particular interest, demonstrating as they do a link with an earlier Irish manuscript tradition. A selection of the Rennes examples are presented in Ills. 9 and 10.

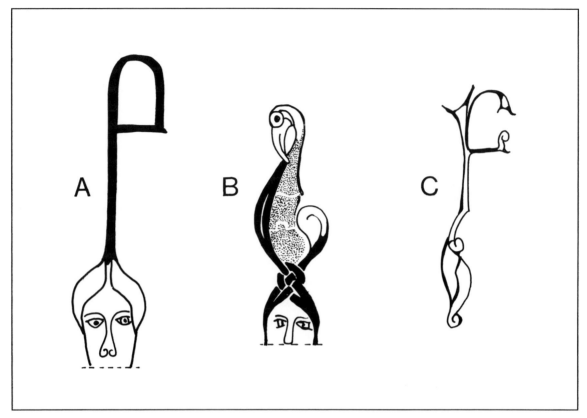

Ill. 9. A selection of illuminated initial letters from the Rennes Manuscript. A and B, featuring anthropomorphic and ornithomorphic elements are from the Patristic Texts section of the manuscript; C is from the section of the manuscript which provides an account of the Life of the Westmeath saint Colman Mac Luacháin (by Rhoda Cronin)

The manuscript also features numerous annotations, pen strokes, traces of prickings and rulings and even traces of rust, suggesting the use of a clasp in its binding which is of sheepskin. Only an approximate date has been assigned to the manuscript, and this is based on both external and internal characteristics. Two distinct hands may be distinguished for the script: one part dates to the late fourteenth or early fifteenth century while another section is of fifteenth-century date. The binding, however, is of eighteenth-century date. It therefore seems that the components of the Rennes Manuscript were brought together during the eighteenth century at the latest.

Contents

The materials contained within the texts are drawn from different periods. For example, the texts by Saint Bernard and the Dindshenchas are twelfth century, those of St Thomas Aquinas are thirteenth century and the text of the Travels of Sir John Mandeville is fourteenth century in date.

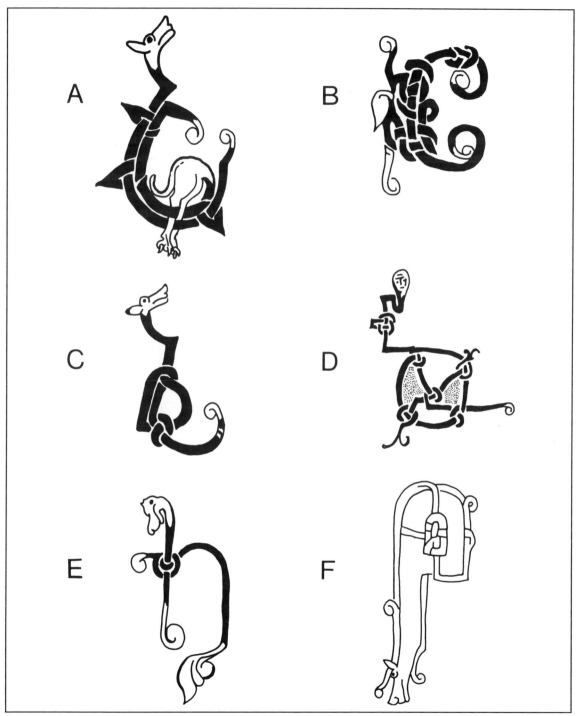

Ill. 10. A selection of illuminated initial letters from the Dindshenchas section of the Rennes Manuscript. Most of these are zoomorphic in style and provide a link with Ireland's Early Medieval manuscript tradition (by Rhoda Cronin)

Patristic Texts (Folios 1-51, 70-73)

This section consists of short religious tracts on Christian virtues and duties, translated into Irish from Latin. The tract on poverty consists of a collection of quotations gathered from the works of Ss Augustine, Bede, Gregory, Jerome and others. There are also collections of notes on the virtues of patience which are based on scripture and on the writings of Augustine, Bernard and Origen. Homilies on the Virgin are attributed to St Bernard, while the sermon on the Eucharist quotes Ambrose, Augustine, John Balbus and Peter Lombard. The treatise on Confession quotes from the great works of St Thomas Aquinas. It begins: 'These are the sixteen conditions that confession requires to have in it . . .' (f. 35a Col. 2). Added to the margin of this section (f. 37b) are the words: 'Scarcely a man in Eirinn makes his confession as this book directs'.

Most of the above texts are published in Latin. It is not known if other Irish versions exist. It has been suggested, based on the evidence of style, language and the sources drawn upon to compile them that the sermons were written by one author and, based on the nature of their contents, that he probably was a Franciscan friar.

The Travels of Sir John Mandeville (Folios 52-69)

According to this text Sir John Mandeville was an English knight who set off on a thirty-four year long period of travel to the Holy Land in 1332. On his return to Rome his book was allegedly confirmed by the Pope. He died at Liège in 1372. There is considerable debate as to how much of the book is original and, indeed, about the true identity of its author. Many manuscript versions exist of his travels and an Irish translation of the original is found in the Rennes manuscript. The first scholar to make known the existence of the Rennes version of this well-known Medieval book was J.H. Todd, who published an account of the manuscript in 1870.

Todd proposed, based on his examination of the preface which begins at f. 52a, Col.2, that the work was translated in 1472 at Rossbroin (now Rossbrin), near Schull, West Cork, by the well-known Irish chieftain and scholar, Finghin Ó Mathgamhna (O'Mahony). He furthermore suggested that this was probably the Finghin referred to by the Four Masters as having died in 1496, and who was described as being a great supporter of 'the humanity and hospitality of West Munster, a wise man, learned in the Latin and the English'. The *Annals of Ulster* also refers to him as a learned man, well-versed in world history.

In 1886, however, John Abercromby disputed Todd's date of 1472 for Finghin O'Mahony's translation and states that it was more likely to be 1475. This is supported by the Egerton Ms. which also features a fifteenth-century version of Mandeville's Travels and refers to the date 1475 for the original translation. Abercromby also went on to dispute Todd's interpretation of the first line of the preface, claiming that it was O'Mahony's original translation which was produced at Rossbroin. Based on a note at the bottom of f. 69 (Pl. 21) he proposed that the Rennes version was written at Kilcrea. The text of this note is:

Pl. 8. An aerial view of Kilcrea friary from the south-east (Photo: Denis Power, Cork Archaeological Survey)

Pl. 9. A view of the sacristy, with the scriptorium above, at Kilcrea.
The large number of windows in the scriptorium would have ensured
that it was a bright room (Photo: Paul Tassie)

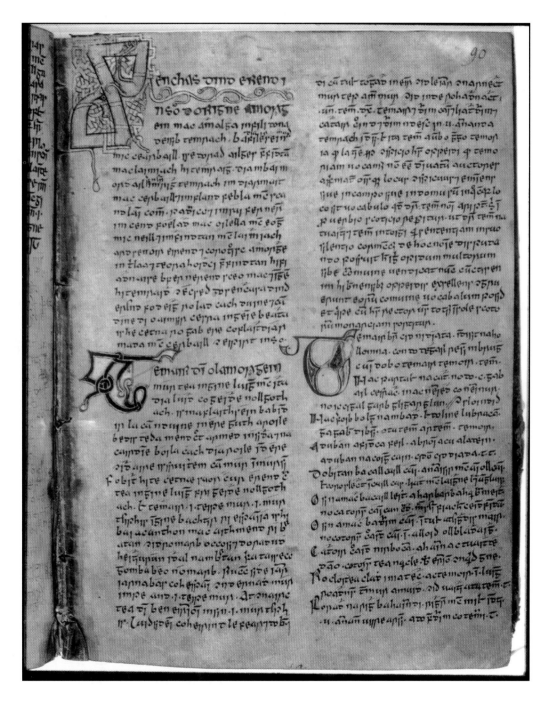

Pl. 10. The first page (Folio 90) of the Dindshenchas section of the Rennes Manuscript. The text is laid out in two columns and features elaborate initial letters. It is written in Irish and consists of a collection of topographical legends in both prose and verse.

(Photo: Bibliothèque Municipale, Rennes)

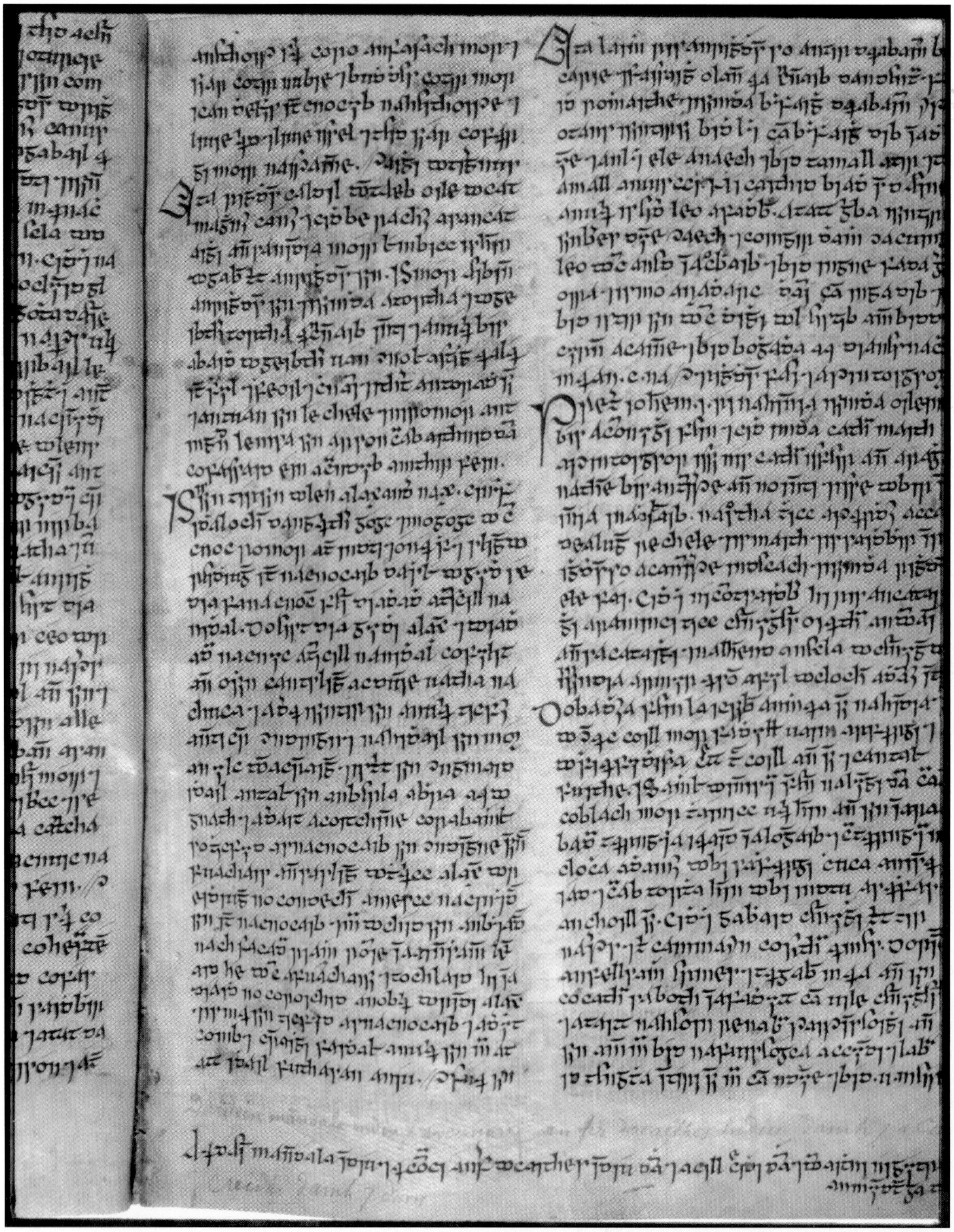

Pl. 11. The final page (Folio 69) of the Travels of Sir John Mandeville, a section of the Rennes Manuscript. At the bottom is a colophon which links the writing of the manuscript with the Kilcrea scriptorium.

(Photo: Bibliothèque Municipale, Rennes)

Dardein manndála indiu ⁊ ar comarci an fir docaithes indiu damh ⁊ a Cill Creidhi damh ⁊ dom aithni ní gúitrengach an muindterga tú.

This was translated by Abercromby as:

Maundy Thursday today and (I am) under protection of the man today that eats an ox and at Cill Crea an ox and to my knowledge thou art no false-fasting (read gutrednach?) unkindly person.

Maundy Thursday was an alternative name for Holy Thursday, and the reference to the writer's patron eating an ox on that day was made in the context of the following day being Good Friday – a fast day. It is generally accepted that the Rennes version of the tale was transcribed shortly after 1475, when the Rossbroin version was written.

A fragment of a Saint's life (Folio 74)

This short section contains an account of the relationship between St Bernard and St Brigid. It also features a note in Irish, which has been translated as follows:

I am Edmond óg O'Kelly who wrote this Latin verse in Baile-Puirt-an Rideri, i.e. in the Glenn, the sixth day of the month of August, 1599; the first year of the war of the Munstermen against the foreigners; and may this plundering fall upon them, if the will of God be with us in making this prayer.

The identification of Baile-Puirt-an-Rideri has been suggested as Glin, Co. Limerick, while the war referred to was the Essex campaign in Munster during the Nine Years War.

A Life of St Colman, son of Luacháin (Folios 75-89)

This section, which occupies fifteen folios, begins in Latin and then continues in Irish. No other copy of this Life is known to exist and there are no marginal notes to suggest where the Rennes copy was written. It was edited and published by the great German celticist Kuno Meyer in 1911.

The St Colman dealt with is said to be Colman son of Luacháin, a seventh-century little known saint who was formerly venerated at Lann (Lann-mic-Luacháin) in Co. Westmeath. The main period of writing the Lives of the Saints was during the eleventh and twelfth centuries. Problems with trying to separate fact from fiction within the texts are inevitable as, by this stage, the saints' lives become almost legendary fiction. It was probably not the intention of the writer to produce an accurate account of St Colman's life. Rather, it is likely that it was written in order to promote his monastery's status, to explain political and social situations, to serve as sermons or sagas or purely to popularise the saint by references to his 'miracles' or to supernatural phenomena that are supposedly associated with him. It is almost certain that the Life of Colman was intended more for popular consumption than to a more fulfilling instructive role.

The more reliable facts give reference to Colman as being born before the end of the sixth century and dying during the last quarter of the seventh century, not far from Portloman on Loch

Owel (near Mullingar). His father's family was descended from the royal race of Conall Cremthainne, while his mother was derived from Echaid Mugmedon, their common ancestor being Niall of the Nine Hostages. Colman is said to have founded several monasteries in Munster, including Cell Uird, Fermoy. It is almost certain that the text was originally written in Co. Westmeath because of the detailed references to the topography of the area contained within it. It can also be suggested with some certainty that it was written after 1122, when, according to the *Annals of Ulster,* his relics were re-discovered.

Dindshenchas (Folios 90-125)

The Dindshenchas is probably the most studied section of the Rennes Manuscript. Work has been published on it by people like Whitley Stokes, E.J. Gwynn, George Petrie, Eoin O'Curry and Kuno Meyer. Dindshenchas (tradition about lore and places) consists of a collection of topographical legends in both prose and verse. Many of the stories behind the history of the place-names are of a folklore type nature. The prose was partially translated by scholars such as Petrie, O'Curry and O'Brady. Whitley Stokes deals more comprehensively with it in *Revue Celtique.* The verse (Metrical Dindshenchas) was examined by E.J. Gwynn. He produced five volumes of material as part of the Todd lecture series published between 1903-35. His work incorporates texts, translations and a commentary on the vocabulary. The Dindshenchas may refer to certain archaeological sites and monuments visible in the tenth century and later. The Rennes copy, for example, refers to forty-two sites and places occurring throughout the country. Included among these are Tara, Co. Meath, Sliabh Mish, Co. Kerry, Beara, Co. Cork, Uisneach, Co. Westmeath and Lough Lene, Co. Kerry. A portion of a reasonably typical example of the type of entry found in the Rennes Dindshenchas is quoted in translation below. It concerns how *Tonn Clidna,* a loud surge in Glandore Bay, Co. Cork, got its name:

This is the time at which the illimitable seaburst arose and spread throughout the regions of the present world. Because there were at that season Erin's three great floods, namely, Clidna's flood and Ladru's flood and Ladru's and Baile's; but none in the same hour did they arise: Ladru's flood was the middle one. The flood pressed on aloft and divided throughout the land of Erin till it caught yon boat and the damsel asleep in it on the beach. So there she was drowned, Clidna the Shapely, Genann's daughter, from whom Tonn Clidna (Clidna's wave) is named.

Stokes suggested that the Rennes Dindshenchas was probably written in the fourteenth or fifteenth century. However, the material for the prose was probably collected in the latter half of the tenth century while that for the verses was compiled in the eleventh or twelfth century. Meyer was also of the same opinion. There is no scribal note, however, to substantiate this suggested date. It is a source of great value to students of Irish folklore and placenames.

Something of the atmosphere of a Medieval Franciscan scriptorium may be felt in the room above the sacristy at Kilcrea, despite it being a roofless ruin. It is quite easy to imagine its well-lit interior, furnished with books and writing paraphernalia, being heated from the large fireplace in the east gable. Its library would have consisted of handwritten manuscripts dealing with religious and devotional topics, as well as historical and quasi-historical treatises. Unfortunately, however, the same historical circumstances which led to the dissolution of the monasteries also eventually led to the scattering of this library's contents. All was not lost, fortunately, for some of the Kilcrea manuscripts finally ended up in safe-keeping in Rennes, Brittany. Today, the Rennes Manuscript serves to demonstrate the important role which was played by Kilcrea friary in promoting and maintaining learning in Ireland during the Medieval period.

Burial Monuments

Introduction

The burial monuments at Kilcrea are all located within the friary buildings. They include head-stones, tombs, a mausoleum, mural plaques and some seventeenth-century grave-slabs. They range in date from 1625 to the 1990s. It should be noted that there would have been few burials located within the walls of the friary during the Medieval period, except for those of the founder and of some important ecclesiastics. According to local tradition the Medieval burial ground was located in the field to the north of the friary. It was only when the complex went out of use as a friary that it became used as a burial place on a regular basis. Today burial still takes place at the friary in certain plots, despite over-crowding, unsanitary conditions and a century of pleas for the friary to be given a rest. One wonders how much longer the structure of the friary can withstand the pressures of continuous burial. Among those commemorated are Cormac Láidir MacCarthy, the friary's founder, Thomas O'Herlihy, Bishop of Ross, Arthur O'Leary, the outlaw, and many of the families from the surrounding areas.

The earliest work carried out on the burial monuments and on those individuals that they commemorate was published in 1912 by Dr Robert Cochrane, an inspector of ancient monuments with the Board of Works. He produced a ground-floor plan of the friary which shows the location of many of the burials. This plan is not annotated, nor is it accompanied by a catalogue. In his report Cochrane refers to the indiscriminate burial practices within the friary. He quotes from two reports, sent to the Board of Works in 1895 from the secretary of the Cork Historical and Archaeological Society, complaining of the unsanitary conditions at the friary arising from the overcrowding of burials. One of these reports stated: 'the abbey is used as a graveyard, which is in a disgraceful condition, it is overcrowded, the coffins are not sunk below the ground . . .'. A former Board of Works' inspector, Sir Thomas Deane, reported after a visit: 'the condition of the graveyard is impossible to describe – coffins over ground, corpses hardly covered. It would be positively dangerous to send work-men there, at any rate in the hot season'. Steps to deal with this situation were taken in 1910-11 when extensive repairs were being carried out to the friary. It was arranged that henceforward burials were

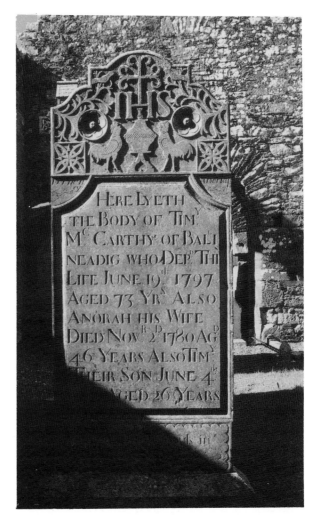

Ill. 11. A fine example of a late eighteenth-century headstone at Kilcrea. It was carved by Hickey's of Aherla, probably the best known family of headstone sculptors in county Cork (Photo: Paul Tassie)

'to be confined to those in the ecclesiastical union of parishes having burial rights within the walls . . .'.

The first analysis of the people and families buried at Kilcrea was published in 1966 by Micheál Ó Murchú as part of the publication marking the quincentenary of the founding of the friary. In the first part of this article some of the better known figures buried at Kilcrea, for example Cormac Láidir MacCarthy and his lineage, Bishop Thomas O'Herlihy, and Fr. Thaddeus O'Sullivan, are dealt with. The second part, which is based on the research of Richard Henchion, makes reference to the early seventeenth-century burial monuments and proceeds to deal with the burials of the clans of the McCarthys, O'Mahonys, Murphys, Delaneys, O'Callaghans and many more. It makes reference to the Hickeys of Aherla, the well-known family of headstone sculptors, and finally it refers to the mausoleum of Martin Hayes.

Ó Murchú's work was followed by the publication of Richard Henchion's article on Kilcrea's burial monuments in the 1968 issue of the *Journal of the Cork Historical and Archaeological Society*. This features a very useful plan to one hundred and forty-two burial monuments within the friary and provides a list of all their inscriptions. In addition, it includes notes on a selection of those monuments and provides an index of stone masons, place-names and personal names associated with the burial monuments in the friary. This valuable publication, which was the result of extensive work, has recorded for posterity many aspects of the social history of Kilcrea.

Who was buried at Kilcrea?

Burial monuments are essentially social documents. The recording of the Kilcrea monuments and their inscriptions is vital in order to advance insights into the political, social and religious aspects of the region. The friary of Kilcrea has buried within its walls the bodies of a variety of people ranging from important ecclesiastical and secular historical figures to members of the landed aristocracy and their tenants as well as the merchant classes. Burial at Kilcrea was not just confined to people from the immediate vicinity. During the seventeenth century burial grounds became overcrowded in Cork city and, as a result, some rural graveyards in its vicinity were chosen for use. For some reason Kilcrea was especially favoured by Catholic members of the merchant classes, and many of the Hayes, Ryan, Connellan and McSwiney families (Henchion nos. 3, 88, 13 and 51) were buried there. Henchion provides some interesting data in his 1968 publication. For example, the two most common place-names occurring on the Kilcrea headstones are Cork city and Ovens. The most common surname was Murphy, followed by McCarthy. The stone masons who were responsible for the majority of the finely carved headstones belonged to the well-known Hickey family of Aherla. This family has been stone-cutters and sculptors for well over two hundred years and its name appears on many of the headstones throughout county Cork.

While it is not feasible to deal with every Kilcrea burial monument and each of the families they commemorate in this book, a selection of the more interesting ones will be dealt with in chronological order.

Cormac McTeige MacCarthy (1411-1494)

Cormac MacCarthy, more popularly known as Cormac Láidir MacCarthy, was born in 1411. He became the ninth lord of Muskerry in 1449 and was the founder of Kilcrea friary. He was also responsible for the building of the tower-house castles at Blarney, Kilcrea and Carrignamuck as well as the nunnery at Ballyvacadane. The *Annals of Ulster* record for the year 1478 that 'Cormac Mag Carthaigh was emasculated by the sons of Diarmuid Mag Carthaigh of the keep and by Cormac, son of Tadhg, son of Cormac'. The *Annals of the Four Masters* record for the year 1495 that he was a 'man who had ordered that the Sabbath should be strictly observed throughout his territory'.

Cormac was wounded at Carrignamuck castle, Dripsey, by his brother Eoghan and by Eoghan's sons. He later died of his wounds and was buried at Kilcrea friary in 1494. Eoghan, who would have been next in line for the lordship, was subsequently dismissed by his clan and Cormac Láidir's son, Cormac Oge, became the next Lord of Muskerry. It is reputed that the following descendants were also buried in the tomb of Cormac Láidir: Cormac Oge McCormac MacCarthy, his son, the tenth Lord of Muskerry (died 1537); Cormac Oge's son, Tadhg, the eleventh lord of Muskerry (died 1565); Tadhg's son, Sir Dermot McTeige MacCarthy, the thirteenth Lord of Muskerry (died 1570), and, finally, Sir Dermot's son, Sir Cormac McDermot MacCarthy, the sixteenth Lord of Muskerry (died 1616).

The tomb of the MacCarthy lords no longer survives today. However, the text of the inscription on Cormac Láidir's tomb was recorded in a seventeenth century manuscript as:

Hic jacet Cormacus filius Thadei Cormaci filii Dermitii Magni mac Carthaigh D. de Musgry flaym as istius coventus primus fundator 1494.

Although local tradition says Cormac was buried in the tomb recess in the north-east corner of the chancel, the seventeenth-century source states that he was buried in the middle of the choir. The tomb recess features a commemorative wall-plaque which was erected in 1966 by the friary's quincentenary committee (Pl. 12).

Bishop Thomas O'Herlihy (died 1579 or 80)

Thomas O'Herlihy was consecrated bishop of Ross, a Cork diocese, in 1561. In 1563 he attended the Council of Trent along with two other Irish bishops. This Council (1545-63) was held in Italy and was the principal organ for the reform of discipline within the Catholic Church. It affiliated papal authority and rejected conciliation with Protestants. In 1569 O'Herlihy was sent to the Catholic courts of Europe and to the Holy See in order to seek aid for the persecuted Catholics of Ireland. On his return he continued to work despite the dangers of being a Catholic bishop in Elizabethan times. He was, however, arrested and handed over to Sir John Perrott in 1571. He was subsequently imprisoned in the Tower of London for about three years. His release was due to the help and influence of Cormac MacTeige MacCarthy. He lived for a brief period with Sir Cormac after his release, but then moved to a small farm in Muskerry. He died in 1579 or 1580 and was buried in Kilcrea. His exact burial spot is not known but he is commemorated by a modern plaque situated in the south-east corner of the chancel.

Fr Thaddeus O'Sullivan (died 1597)

Fr O'Sullivan was well-known as a preacher throughout Ireland. His travels also involved charitable missions. He was advisor to Dermot Gray, Bishop of Cork. In 1597, while on one of his missions, he became ill and died. An interesting story is told of the events surrounding his burial. It was not a safe time for Catholics to carry out burials at Kilcrea as English troops were garrisoned at the nearby tower house. To avoid danger the funeral took place at night. The multiplicity of by-roads and the darkness made the task of finding the friary difficult. The story records that it was left to a horse's instincts to find the way to the friary. The horse successfully brought the remains to the friary in the early hours of the morning and it is said that Fr O'Sullivan was buried in the east of the cloister at the chapter-room door.

Fr Matthew O'Leyn (died 1590 or 1599)

There is little recorded in the historical sources about Fr O'Leyn except for the events surrounding his death. In 1599 there was a surprise attack on Kilcrea by English soldiers. Many of the friars fled for their lives but Fr O'Leyn, who was 67 years old, failed to escape. He was stabbed in the back while trying to cross a ford in the river Bride. The year of his death is also recorded as 1590.

Fr Felix McCarthy

Felix McCarthy distinguished himself by his charity and hospitality to all those he encountered. His life was to change, however, after he stabbed his blood brother to death during a quarrel. Overcome with remorse, he denounced the world and sought permission to join the Franciscan Order. After many refusals because of his evil deed, he was eventually received. It is said that after he was ordained he lost the use of all fingers except those required for celebrating the Eucharist. His brethren accepted this as a sign of God's mercy. It is also recorded in local tradition that at the time of his death the entire friary was seen to light up in flames. This was taken as a sign that Fr McCarthy had at last achieved peace.

Seventeenth-Century Grave-Slabs

A small number of seventeenth-century grave-slabs occur within the friary, surviving in varying fragmentary conditions. As stated above the earliest known monument dates to 1625. The next earliest is 1626.

Ills. 12(a) and 14

This rectangular slab is located in a plain tomb niche in the north-east corner of the nave. It survives in good condition except for one crack which occurs beneath the cross-head. The design, which is carved in relief, consists of an interlaced cross-head surmounting a shaft which terminates in a stepped base. There is no evidence to suggest that this slab bore an inscription.

Ill. 12(b)

This consists of portion of the cross-head of a slab. It features the remains of a seven-armed wheeled cross-head, carved in relief. The letters 'IHS' are carved within a small circle at the centre of the design. There is no surviving evidence of an inscription.

Ill. 12(c)

This tapered slab is presently standing upside down towards the northwestern end of the nave, and only its stepped base is visible. The accompanying illustration is based on a drawing by Westropp who visited the friary in 1908. The drawing is preserved in the Royal Irish Academy and is accompanied by a note: 'monumental slab buried upside down as a headstone' (RIA Ms. 3 A 52 201). The design, which is incised, consists of a seven-armed wheeled cross. The cross-shaft terminates in a stepped base and the base of the slab is of rounded form. There is no evidence to suggest that it bore an inscription.

Ill. 13(a)

This consists of portion of a slightly tapered slab. All that remains of the design, carved in relief, are the two lower arm-terminals of the cross-head and portion of the cross-shaft which features three cross-bands. There are the remains of a raised border on both sides of the slab. There is no evidence to suggest that it bore an inscription.

Ill. 13(b)

This consists of the upper portion of a rectangular slab. The design, which is carved in relief, consists of a seven-armed wheeled cross with a fleur-de-lis at each arm terminal. The upper portion of the cross-shaft is also preserved. There is no surviving evidence for an inscription.

Ill. 13(c)

This fragmentary slab survives in three portions: two upper and one lower. It was of rectangular shape and featured a seven-armed wheeled cross, carved in relief and terminating in a stepped base. A small plain Latin cross, carved in relief, occurs on the sinister side of the cross-shaft, immediately below the cross-head. An inscription occurs on the dexter and sinister sides and on the upper dexter corner. It reads:

WI. MS ...... 1625 / O:M:T:S: / TE:O ... W:M:T:S:

Richard Henchion suggests that this may be identified as a McSweeney grave-marker and that the initials on it stand for Owen McTirrelagh Swvny and William McTirrelagh Swvny. He also states that there were several Tirrelagh McSwvnys among the military followers of the McCarthys in the seventeenth century.

Ill. 13(d)

This consists of a rectangular slab which is badly broken at its top. The design, which is incised, consists of a lozenge-shaped cross-head enclosing a plain cross. The cross-shaft terminates in a stepped base. The letters 'IHS' are carved in relief on the dexter side of the cross-shaft. An inscription survives on the sinister and dexter sides of the slab and reads:

(C?)OK(L?).ECUNIGAUL. / (Q?)UIF(I°?) 1626

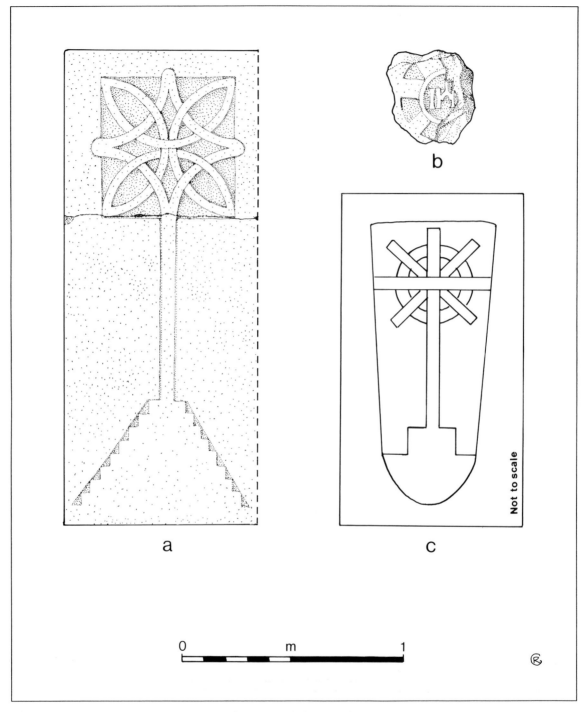

Ill. 12. Seventeenth-century grave-slabs from Kilcrea. Such slabs, which feature a variety of cross-forms, may have marked graves or served as tomb lids. The example on the left, (a), is located in a tomb niche in the nave (by Rhoda Cronin)

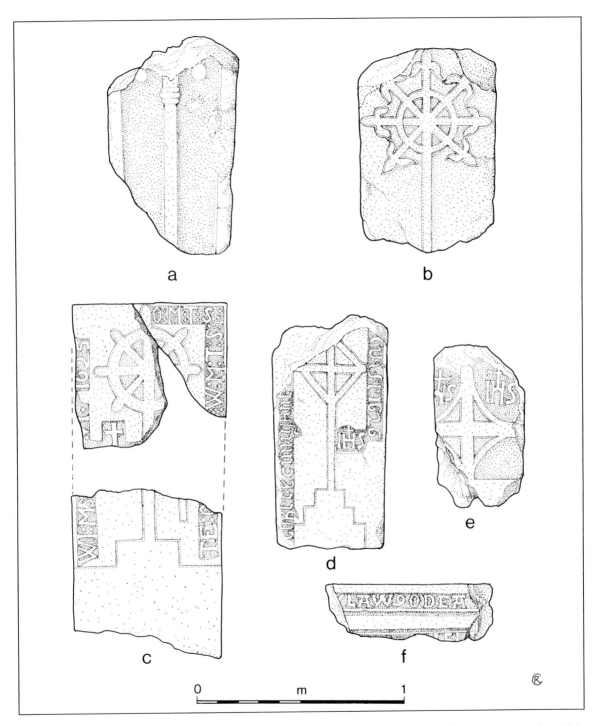

Ill. 13. A further selection of seventeenth-century grave-slabs from Kilcrea, some of which feature inscriptions. The example at bottom left, (c), is dated to 1625 and may commemorate the McSweeneys (by Rhoda Cronin)

Ill. 14. A tomb niche, complete with grave-slab, in the north-east corner of the friary's nave. The slab bears no inscription but burial in tomb niches was usually reserved for important people (Photo: Paul Tassie)

Ill. 13(e)

This consists of portion of a slab which features a cross-head carved in relief. It consists of a lozenge-shaped cross-head enclosing a Latin cross. The letters 'IHS' occur beside both upper external angles of the cross-head. There is no surviving evidence for an inscription.

Ill. 13(f)

This small portion of a slab features only part of an inscription. It reads:

. LAW9 O DEA

Arthur O'Leary (1747-1773)

The best-known burial monument at Kilcrea is undoubtedly that of Arthur O'Leary. He was born in 1747 at Raleigh, near Macroom, and died in 1773 after having been shot by an English soldier at Carriganima, County Cork.

He was educated in France and subsequently joined the Hungarian Hussars, serving under the Empress Marie Thérése. He distinguished himself by his valour on the field and achieved high rank. He returned to Ireland bringing with him his favourite horse, described as a brown mare. In 1767 he married Eibhlín Dhubh Ní Chonaill of Derrynane, County Kerry, against the wishes of her mother, Máire Dhubh. Eibhlín was aunt of Daniel O'Connell, the Liberator. Her mother, who was a keeper of the old traditional ways, was a well-known *bean caointe* in the area.

Art O'Leary had considerable property, was strong spirited and above all, courageous. All of these attributes combined to excite the jealousy of Mr Abraham Morris, the High-Sherriff in the Macroom district.

There are various accounts of the events that led to Art O'Leary's death. It is not clear which of these is the true one, though all are centred on the bitter enmity that existed between O'Leary and Morris. The first account comes from the historical notes of Dr Caulfield, the seventeenth-century Cork antiquarian. In these Caulfield records that O'Leary's horse led the field at the Muskerry Hunt. Morris, who was enraged at the display of a Catholic's horse leading the field, offered O'Leary £5 for the horse. At that time the Penal Laws were in full force and one of these, a statute of William III, forbade a Catholic to keep or have a horse which exceeded £5 in value. Morris attempted to humiliate O'Leary by his offer. O'Leary refused it and a brawl followed. A meeting of the magistrates was arranged and O'Leary was declared an outlaw. A short time later, while riding his horse near Carriganima, he was shot by a soldier under the command of Morris. O'Leary returned fire, but a second shot from the soldier killed him. He fell from his horse, who returned back to his dwelling house at Raleigh.

Another account of Art O'Leary's death, which is quite similar in most respects to the above one, was told by Cornelius O'Leary, the outlaw's son, to Abraham Abell who later related it to John Windele. In this account O'Leary's horse won a race at Macroom, a race in which Morris' horse was also involved in. A similar sequence of events to those outlined above then followed.

A third version of O'Leary's death is recorded in Halls' *Ireland: Its Scenery and Character*. In this the authors state that the dispute between Morris and O'Leary was over priority in receiving a drink of water from an old woman at a spring. O'Leary struck Morris and was forced to stand trial. He absconded and escaped abroad. He was then proclaimed an outlaw. After some time he returned home where he made no attempt to disguise himself. He was eventually shot dead by a group of soldiers.

The final version of O'Leary's death is contained in a pamphlet by Michael Pyne, dating to the early nineteenth century and reproduced in 1905. The account is as follows: Morris was at Drishane castle with a Dominic Harding. O'Leary and Morris engaged in a dispute previously. O'Leary knew that Morris was at Drishane and was determined to meet him on his way home to try and settle this matter. He visited Daniel Reardon Barrett's house in the village of Carriganima for a few drinks and then continued on his way to Drishane despite the efforts of

Reardon to persuade him to turn back. Meanwhile a warning had reached Drishane about O'Leary and a group of soldiers were quickly rounded up and sent to Carriganima. O'Leary was fatally shot on his horse by a soldier under Morris' direct order.

Pyne mentions in his pamphlet that he received the above information from Jeffrey O'Herlihey, of Macroom, and from a farmer, Daniel Hugh Keller, who was supposed to have been an eye-witness to the event.

There are common themes in the various accounts outlined above. Firstly, there appears to have existed a strong animosity between O'Leary and Morris for some time. Secondly, O'Leary's horse performed well in public against Morris's horse (either at the Macroom races or the Muskerry hunt). Morris, because of his role as High Sherriff, was in a position to use the law to his advantage. This he did, eventually causing O'Leary's death.

Morris was tried for the killing of Art O'Leary, but was honourably acquitted. It is also recorded that shortly after O'Leary's death his brother attempted to kill Morris. Morris was in lodgings in Hammond's Marsh in Cork city and was badly wounded having been shot through a window. O'Leary fled and escaped to America.

The Lament

The story of Art O'Leary would probably never have achieved such fame was it not for *Caoineadh Airt Uí Laoighaire (Lament for Art O'Leary)* extemporised by his wife, Eibhlín Dhubh, over his dead body. This late eighteenth-century poem was described by Ó Tuama and Kinsella as a 'masterpiece in the lyric "keening" tradition' and as one of the 'great laments and one of the great love poems of the Irish language.' It is still preserved in the oral tradition in parts of counties Cork and Kerry. Two extracts of a translation of this epic poem are quoted below. Firstly Eibhlín Dhubh outlines Art's ancestry and describes some of the places associated with him:

> *My friend and my calf!*
> *O Art Ó Laoghaire*
> *son of Conchúr son of Céadach*
> *son of Laoiseach Ó Laoighaire:*
> *West from the Gaortha*
> *and East from the Caolchnoc*
> *where the berries grow,*
> *yellow nuts on the branches*
> *and masses of apples*
> *in their proper season*
> *– need anyone wonder*
> *if Uí Laoghaire were alight*
> *and Béal Átha an Ghaorthaigh*

> *and Gúgán the holy*
> *for the fine-handed rider*
> *who used tire out the hunt*
> *as they panted from Greanach*
> *and the slim hounds gave up?*

Then she begins her curse on Morris, the man responsible for Art's death:

> *Ruin and bad cess to you,*
> *ugly traitor Morris,*
> *who took the man of my house*
> *and father of my young ones*
> *– a pair walking the house*
> *and the third in my womb,*
> *and I doubt that I'll bear it.*

O'Leary was initially buried at Kilnamartra cemetery, the burial place of the Tuath na Dromann. Six months later his body was moved to Kilcrea and was buried in a tomb which still stands in the south-east corner of the nave, beneath the tower. Henchion read its inscription (Pl. 13) as:

> *Lo, Arthur Leary, Genrous*
> *Handsome, Brave, Slain in*
> *his Bloom, Lies in this Humble*
> *Grave. Died May 4th 1773*
> *Aged 26 years.*

> *Having served the Empress Maria*
> *Theresa as Captain of Hungarian Hussars*
> *he returned home to be outlawed and treacherously*
> *Shot by Order of the British Government, His sole crime*
> *Being that he refused to part with a favourite horse*
> *For the sum of five pounds*

> *Cornelius O'Leary, Barrister-at*
> *Law, ex-Captain of the Gardes-Francaises, son of Arthur the Outlaw,*
> *born August 28 A.D. 1768, died*
> *August 20 A.D. 1846. C. F. Purcell O'Leary, Barrister-at-Law*
> *Son of Cornelius, Born October 6 A.D.*
> *1815 died June 21 A.D. 1846*

It is said that the remains of another grandson, Dr Goodwin Purcell O'Leary, MA, Professor of *materia medica* in Queen's College Cork were also interred here.

William O'Brien (1727–1793)

An interesting story surrounds the grave of William O'Brien which is situated at the west end of the south aisle of the church. It is said that he was a priest and that rounds were made at his grave because of his pious reputation. Henchion was unable to trace such a priest in the historical records for the period. He did, however, suggest the possibility that the origins of the rounds lay with a Fr William O'Brien, P.P. of Ovens and Aglish, who died 1816 or 17. He also suggests that this priest was the son of the William O'Brien whose name is recorded on this monument.

In the opening chapter the historical sources for Kilcrea friary were outlined. These were seen as being rather limited in their scope, combining to deliver only a brief overview of the history of the friary. The evidence of Kilcrea's burial monuments and their inscriptions, however, is different. Through them the visitor comes into direct contact with some of the people whose lives were touched by history and who made history. The most important of these include Cormac MacCarthy, Gaelic chieftain and founder of the friary, Bishop O'Herlihy, Catholic bishop of the Reformation period, and Art O'Leary, noble victim of the Penal Laws and the subject of the greatest lament known from Irish literature. The hundreds of other burial monuments at Kilcrea remind the visitor of the strong links that have existed between this historic place and the people of the district over the centuries.

Envoi

This book has explored several aspects of the Franciscan friary at Kilcrea. The ideals which gave rise to the foundation of the Franciscan Order were outlined and a brief history of the Order in Ireland was sketched. Unfortunately, the history of the Kilcrea friary itself is incomplete. Little is known about St Cere who founded the first Christian establishment at the site, but who is commemorated forever in the name of the Medieval friary.

The history of the friary is intertwined with that of Cormac Láidir MacCarthy and his descendants. The trials and tribulations of this family during the conquest of Munster by the English are matched by the many turbulent events which took place within the friary's cloisters. Yet, for centuries after the last of the MacCarthys was buried in the family tomb in the church the Franciscan tradition remained alive in the ruins of the friary. History records that this was so up until the 1880s.

Various historical personages are associated with Kilcrea. Included amongst these are the leaders of the MacCarthy clan, Bishop Thomas O'Herlihy, who represented Ireland at the Council of Trent, the famous preaching friar Thaddeus O'Sullivan, and Matthew O'Leyn, a little-known elderly friar who was murdered by English soldiers in 1599. However, undoubtedly the most famous person associated with the friary is the eighteenth-century outlaw Art O'Leary. This is largely because he was the subject of one of the greatest laments ever written in the Irish language.

The existence of *Caoineadh Airt Uí Laoighaire* adds poignancy to the ruins of Kilcrea, but it is not the only literature associated with this friary. The ruins of the Medieval Franciscan library and scriptorium still stand outside the chancel and form one of the more interesting aspects of the friary. In it were housed Gaelic and Latin manuscripts dealing with the subjects of religion, history and tradition. Only one of these has survived the vicissitudes of time. It is now housed in the Bibliothèque Municipale at Rennes, Brittany. Its illuminated letters, as well as some of its contents, hark back to an earlier monastic age. Its existence demonstrates the important role played by the Kilcrea scriptorium in recording and promoting learning in Medieval Ireland.

Practically nothing is known about the furnishings of the friary. Historical records convey to us how these were plundered and destroyed by English soldiers during the period of the Reformation. Through chance, however, a splendid ivory crucifixion figure which may have been associated with the friary, has survived. Together with the Kilcrea reliquary it gives an impression of how wonderful the church furnishings must have been.

It is hoped that this book will increase visitors' appreciation of the ruins of Kilcrea and the story behind them. It is a story which also holds true for many other monastic ruins in Ireland. However, there is something special about Kilcrea which always entrances the visitor.

1465-1965

I nÐílċuiṁne AR
Cormac Láiḋir Mac Cárċaiṡ
Tiarna Múscraí
an ċé a ḃunaiṡ an ṁainisċir seo
ḋ'Orḋ Proinsias
aṡus a ċuir faoi ċoiṁirce ḃríḋe í
ḋ'eaṡ 1494
ṡura sona ḋe a anam a ḃea-ḃearċ.
Coisċe Cuiṁneaċáin 1965 - 1966
a ċóṡ an lia ós a leaċċ

Pl. 12. The commemorative wall plaque to the friary's founder, Cormac Láidir MacCarthy, erected in 1966. The tomb in which he was buried no longer survives.

(Photo: Paul Tassie)

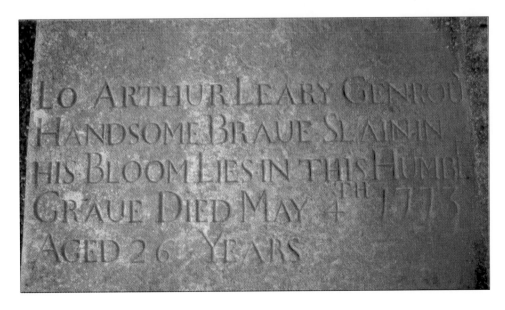

Lo Arthur Leary Genrou
Handsome Braue Slain in
His Bloom Lies in This Humbl
Graue Died May 4th 1773
Aged 26 Years

Pl. 13. The opening lines of the inscription of Art O'Leary's tomb. O'Leary was an eighteenth-century outlaw about whom the famous lament *Caoineadh Art Uí Laoighaire* was composed

(Photo: Paul Tassie)

Pl. 14. The Kilcrea crucifixion figure. This splendid carving is of ivory and was found near Kilcrea during the first half of the nineteenth century.
(Photo: John Sheehan)

Pl. 15. The crucifixion figure is carved with
great attention given to anatomical
detail. It is probably of Italian, early
seventeenth-century workmanship.
(Photo: John Sheehan)

Pl. 16. This nineteenth-century lithograph illustrates one of the few *Agnus Dei* amulet reliquaries from Ireland. It was apparently found in the friary in the late 1840s (Photo: Royal Society of Antiquaries of Ireland)

APPENDIX ONE
The Kilcrea Crucifixion Figure

This crucifixion figure is made of ivory. It is a splendid example of its type, being exquisitely carved with great attention given to anatomical detail (Pls. 14 and 15). The right arm is missing and the left arm is detached. All of the fingers and toes have been broken off, though one thumb survives. The figure wears a loin cloth and its feet are positioned side by side. It is not carved from a single piece of ivory, the arms and the hanging folds of the loin cloth being separate pieces attached to the torso by minute wooden tenons.

The crucifixion figure is presently housed in the museum of the Franciscan friary at Multyfarnham, Co. Westmeath. It was originally donated to the friary at Liberty Street, Cork, on October 7th, 1946, by a Mr Danckart – a member of a long-established Cork family. In 1975 it was deposited on loan in the National Museum of Ireland, where it was examined by Catríona Macleod. Unfortunately, no record of her findings are known to exist in the National Museum's archives. Sometime during the 1980s the object was transferred from Cork to the Franciscan museum at Multyfarnham.

Some documentation concerning the crucifixion figure is contained in the Franciscan Library at Killiney. Included amongst this is a letter, dated May 23rd, 1975, from Fr Benignus Millett, OFM, Killiney, to Fr Florence MacCarthy, OFM, Cork. It was written two months after Macleod's inspection of the object in the National Museum and records her view that it is of Italian workmanship and is of early seventeenth century date. This can be substantiated by the striking parallels, particularly in the treatment of the loin cloth and the close attention to anatomical detail, that exist between the Kilcrea figure and the well-known example, dated to 1630-1, by the German sculptor Georg Petel.

More importantly, the Killiney documentation contains a typed transcription of the text of an 'old pencilled note' which was contained in a box with the crucifixion figure while it was in Cork friary. (Unfortunately, the original note now appears to be lost). The text commences: *This crucifix is almost 400 years old. It was found in a bog near the ruins of the Franciscan Abbey of Kilcrea, County Cork . . .* Further in the text it is stated: *This was many years afterwards discovered and for over a hundred years is in the possession of the family of the present owner* (presumably the Danckerts). The importance of this note is that it indicates that the crucifix figure was found near Kilcrea sometime during the first half of the nineteenth century. This association between the object and Kilcrea's vicinity is repeated in the caption to a photograph of it which is kept in the library of the Franciscan friary in Cork city. This states: *This ivory crucifix was found in a field near Kilcrea abbey about 150 years ago, and was presented to the Franciscan Fathers by Mr Danckert. October 7th 1946.* Of course it cannot be stated unequivocally that the ivory crucifixion figure ever formed part of the religious possession of Kilcrea, though it seems likely that it may have.

An interesting but unlikely theory equates the Kilcrea ivory with a crucifix which was noted by Donatus Mooney as being in the friary in 1584, when English troops raided it. Mooney's account of this event (translated on pp. 8–9) is contained in a manuscript which he wrote in Louvain during 1616-1617 (now held in the Bibliothèque Royale in Brussels, where it is registered as Ms. 3947). The theory that the ivory figure belongs to the 1584 cross is expounded at length in the above-mentioned note, now lost, which was formerly kept with the ivory. It states:

In the year 1584 Elizabeth was then trying to stamp out the Catholic Faith in Ireland, and a company of English soldiers marauding through the district entered the Franciscan monastery and church of Kilcrea. Intent on plunder they demolished the statues and paintings and laid their hands on the sacred utensils. At that time the church possessed a beautiful representation of the crucifixion – a rare work of art indeed. At each extremity of the cross there was a beautiful medallion of the evangelists wrought in gold and silver. Stimulated by a desire to seize the precious metal the soldiers began to quarrel among themselves, and in this brawl they turned their swords against each other till two of them fell mortally wounded. The gold and silver glutted the greed of the survivors and that noble work of art was lost to the convent forever. But the beautiful ivory figure they doubtless regarded as a papist idol and threw it away having wrenched it from the cross which with its gold and silver medallions they carried off as plunder. The figure was found and hidden in a bog close by as was the custom in those troubled days in Ireland when many valuables were hidden in bogs to preserve them from plunder.

It is quite clear, however, that the ivory crucifixion figure from Kilcrea cannot be equated with the Kilcrea crucifix described in some detail by Mooney. There are a number of reasons for this. Firstly, ivory figures were not generally mounted on metal crosses. Secondly, the ivory figure is later in date than the metal crucifix (which is only known from a seventeenth-century account of a sixteenth-century event). Thirdly, in his account of the 1584 raid on Kilcrea, Donatus Mooney does not say that the figure on the cross was of ivory. Instead he describes an object which seems to be typical of sixteenth-century Irish metalwork crucifixes. It may be safely concluded that there is no connection between the ivory figure found near Kilcrea and the metal crucifix from the friary which was defaced by English soldiers in 1584.

APPENDIX TWO
The Kilcrea Reliquary

This oval silver reliquary is *c*.6.4cm long and *c*.5.6cm wide. On the reverse face is a depiction of the crucifixion which is surrounded by the inscription *IN HOC SIGNUM VINSET* (With this Sign He will Conquer). On the front face is a depiction of the *Agnus Dei* with the inscription *ECCE BENEDICTUS AGNUS DEI* (Behold the Blessed Lamb of God). The edges of both its faces are decorated with a rope-moulding effect and feature loops for attachment.

This reliquary was apparently found in Kilcrea friary. It formed part of the private collection of John Lindsey, the Cork antiquarian, and its present provenance is unknown. The sole surviving evidence for the object is contained within the text of a letter written by Lindsay, dated May 5th, 1851, which is preserved in one of G.V. Du Noyer's sketch-books. This forms part of the manuscript collection of the Royal Society of Antiquaries of Ireland. The relevant section of this letter reads as follows:

The Reliquary . . . was found as I was informed at Kilcrea abbey, Co. Cork I think 2 or 3 years since but have no other authority for the appropriation than that of the silversmith from whom I purchased it. I think its age is about the latter part of the 15th century . . .

Accompanying this letter is a lithograph of several antiquities, amongst which is a representation of the reliquary (Pl. 16). The practice of encasing sacred relics in reliquaries in Ireland dates back to the introduction of Christianity during the fifth century. The cult of relics was particularly strong during the eighth and eleventh/twelfth centuries, but continued into the Later Medieval period. Many relics were believed to have power to effect miraculous cures.

The Kilcrea object is a particular form of amulet reliquary known as an *Agnus Dei*. Such capsule-shaped reliquaries were of widespread occurrence throughout Europe during the fifteenth and sixteenth centuries. *Agnus Dei* amulet reliquaries usually had the image of the *Agnus Dei* engraved or repoussé on their front covers. The Kilcrea example seems to have been executed in repoussé. They were made to enshrine a relic made from the wax of the Paschal candle which was blessed each year by the Pope in Rome. The relic was in the form of a circle of wax which was stamped with the image of the *Agnus Dei*.

Reliquaries of this type seem to have been intended for private devotion, and were usually worn as pendants or talismen around the neck. The side and bottom loops on the Kilcrea example may have been used to hold suspended medals. Only a small number of *Agnus Dei* reliquaries are known from Ireland.

Sources

The principal sources which have been used in writing this book are listed below under the appropriate chapter headings. This is not intended to be a comprehensive bibliography for Kilcrea friary. Rather, it aims at providing pointers towards the more widely available, secondary, published sources relevant to various aspects of Kilcrea.

The Franciscans and Kilcrea

For a comprehensive account of the history and development of the Franciscan Order see: Moorman, J., *A History of the Franciscan Order*, Oxford, 1968. The history of the Franciscans in Ireland is dealt with by Conlan, P., *Franciscan Ireland*, Mullingar, 1988. Useful sources for the ecclesiastical and political background of Medieval Ireland include, Watt, J., *The Church in Medieval Ireland*, Dublin, 1972, and Otway-Ruthven, A.J., *A History of Medieval Ireland*, London, 1968. Summary notes on the historical sources for each Medieval foundation in Ireland, including Kilcrea, are contained in Gwynn, A. and Hadcock, R.N., *Medieval Religious Houses: Ireland*, Dublin, 1970. Various aspects of Kilcrea and its history are included in Ó Murchú, M. (ed.), *Kilcrea Through Five Centuries: 1465-1965*, Cork, 1966. The sole published reference to the lead chalice found at Kilcrea is contained in *Sotheby's Catalogue, 7/12/1868, Lot 5*.

The Architecture of Kilcrea

The earliest comprehensive account of Kilcrea and its architecture is Westropp, T.J., The monastery of St Brigid, Kilcrea, and the castle of the MacCarthys, *Journal of the Cork Historical and Archaeological Society*, 16 (1908), 157-177. Shortly afterwards a descriptive account, complete with useful plans and elevations, was published by Cochrane, R., Notes on the structures in the county of Cork vested in the Board of Works for preservation as Ancient Monuments, *Journal of the Cork Historical and Archaeological Society*, 18 (1912), 57-66. The Kilcrea friary features in a suite of papers by Mooney, C., Franciscan Architecture in pre-Reformation Ireland, *Journal of the Royal Society of Antiquaries of Ireland*, 85 (1955), 133-173, 86 (1956), 125-169; 87 (1957), 1-38, 103-124. The most recent descriptive account of the friary is contained in Power, D. et al, *Archaeological Inventory of County Cork, 3*, Dublin, 1997.

Franciscan Writings and the Rennes Manuscript

Fr C. Mooney published a number of papers and books on the Medieval libraries and writings of the Irish Franciscans. These include: Irish Franciscan libraries of the past, *Irish Ecclesiastical Record*, 60 (1942), 215-228; Some Medieval writings of the Irish Franciscans, *Irish Library Bulletin*, 3 (1942), 16-18, and *Devotional Writings of the Irish Franciscans*, 1224-1950, Killiney, 1952. Information on Franciscan writings is also included in Cotter, F.J., *The Friars Minor in Ireland From their Arrival to 1400*, New York, 1994, and Clabby, T., *The Franciscans in Ireland 1400-1534*, unpublished PhD thesis, National University of Ireland,

Galway (1998). No facsimile edition of the Rennes manuscript has been published, nor has a comprehensive study of it appeared. A number of papers which deal with sections or aspects of it, however, have been published. These include: Todd, J.H., Some account of the Irish Ms. deposited by the President de Robien in the Public Library of Rennes, *Proceedings of the Royal Irish Academy, Irish Mss Series,* 1 (1870), 66-81; Abercromby, J., Two Irish fifteenth century versions of Sir John Mandeville's Travels, *Revue Celtique,* 7 (1886), 66-79, 210-224, 358-368; Phillips, J.R., *The Medieval Expansion of Europe,* Oxford, 1988; Stokes, W., The prose tales in the Rennes Dindshenchas, *Revue Celtique,* 15 (1894), 272-336, and, Meyer, K., *Betha Colmáin Mac Lúacháin* (Todd Lecture Series), Dublin, 1911.

Burial Monuments

Interesting information about the formerly poor condition of the cemetery at Kilcrea is contained in Cochrane, R., Notes on the structures in the county of Cork vested in the Board of Works for preservation as Ancient Monuments, *Journal of the Cork Historical and Archaeological Society,* 18 (1912) 57-66. A detailed catalogue of the burial monuments at the friary, complete with a plan and analysis as well as notes on the more interesting inscriptions, is published by Henchion, R., The gravestone inscriptions of county Cork – II, *Journal of the Cork Historical and Archaeological Society,* 73 (1968), 1-30. The historical backgrounds of a number of the more important personages buried at Kilcrea are dealt with in Ó Murchú, M. (ed.), *Kilcrea Through Five Centuries: 1465-1965,* Cork, 1966. Historical information about the MacCarthys, including their connection with the friary, is included in Webb-Gillman, H., Carrignamuck castle, county Cork: a stronghold of the MacCarthys, *Journal of the Cork Historical and Archaeological Sociey* 1 (1892), 11-19, and Sir Cormac McTeige MacCarthy and the sept lands of Muskerry, *Journal of the Cork Historical and Archaeological Society,* 1 (1892), 193-200. An account of the death of Fr Felix McCarthy is included in Meehan, C.P., *The Rise and Fall of the Irish Franciscan Monasteries,* Dublin/London, 1869, while the events which led to the death of Fr Matthew O'Leyn in 1584 are recorded in Mooney, D., Brussels Ms. 3947, published in *Analecta Hibernica,* 6 (1934), 12-138 (ed. B. Jennings). A brief account of the life of Bishop O'Herlihy, buried at Kilcrea *c.*1580, is published by Burke, J., Bishop O'Herlihy, *Journal of the Cork Historical and Archaeological Society,* 26 (1920), 82-83. Information about Art O'Leary and his death is contained in Collins, J.T., Arthur O'Leary, the outlaw, *Journal of the Cork Historical and Archaeological Society,* 54 (1949), 1-7 and 55 (1950), 21-24, and in Hall, A.M. & S.C., *Ireland: Its Scenery and Character,* Dublin, 1841-43. The translated extract from *Caoineadh Airt Uí Laoighaire is* taken from Ó Tuama, S. & Kinsella, T., *An Dunaire 1600-1900: Poems of the Dispossessed,* Dublin, 1981.

The Kilcrea Crucifixion Figure

Manuscript information pertaining to the Kilcrea ivory is filed under *Mss Friaries, Cork* in the Franciscan Library, Killiney. The Georg Petel figure is published in Schiller, G., *Iconography of Christian Art,* 2 (1972), Catalogue no. 494, London.

The Kilcrea Reliquary

This reliquary is briefly noted in Crawford, H.S., A descriptive list of Irish shrines and reliquaries, *Journal of the Royal Society of Antiquaries of Ireland,* 52 (1923), 74-97.

Glossary

Ambulatory – A roofed or vaulted walk or passage around a cloister.

Anthropomorphic – In human form.

Arcade – A range of arches carried on piers or columns

Aumbry – A cupboard in the thickness of a wall, generally near to an altar.

Chamfer – A splayed or bevelled edge made by cutting away the sharp edge of a stone block.

Chancel – The eastern arm of a church in which the main altar is placed; sometimes divided from the NAVE by an archway known as the chancel arch.

Chapter Room – A room set apart in monasteries for the daily meetings of the monks and in which a chapter of the Rule of the Order was read.

Cloister – A quadrangle surrounded by an AMBULATORY connecting the church with the domestic parts of a Medieval monastery.

Colophon – Passage appearing at the end of a manuscript, recording information about the text, place and date of execution, and occasionally the name of scribe.

Conventual – term applied to the non-reform group within the Franciscan Order, which split into two groups in the sixteenth century. This Order died out in Ireland after the Reformation.

Corbel – A stone projecting from a wall in order to support roof timbers, wall shafts and arches.

Course – A continuous, usually horizontal, layer of building material, such as stone, brick, etc.

Dexter – Of or located on the right hand side and therefore on the viewer's left.

Domus Necessarium – A polite term for a Medieval lavatory.

Embrasure – The openings in a parapet wall bewteen the **Merlons;** the recesses for doorways and windows.

Friary – Generally used to mean any place where friars lived.

Garderobe – A Medieval lavatory delivering through a shaft, usually into a pit, drain or fosse.

Hood-Mould – A projecting moulding, to throw off the rain, on the face of the wall above an arch, doorway or window.

Initial – Emphasised letter at the beginning of a text.

Jamb – The straight side of an archway, window or doorway, usually vertical but sometimes inclined.

Joggled – A notching of the voussoirs of an arch or of the stones of a lintel to prevent them sliding.

Light – Opening between the **Mullions or Jambs.**

Lintel – Horizontal beam over a door or window.

Loop – A small narrow Light.

Mullion – An upright between the **Lights** of a window.

Nave – The main body of a church, assigned to the laity.

Observant – Term applied to the reform group within the Franciscan Order in the fifteenth century. The term also applies to that group when the Order split in the sixteenth century. The term ceased *c.*1700.

Piscina – A basin for washing the sacred vessels. It is provided with a drain and is usually set in a small niche in the wall of a sanctuary or chapel near to and south of the altar.

Refectory – The hall in which meals were taken in a monastic establishment.

Sacristy – The room in which sacred vessels and vestments are kept.

Scriptorium – A room set apart in a monastery for writing. They sometimes also functioned as libraries.

Springing point – The point from which an arch springs.

Tracery – The decorative intersecting pattern in the upper part of a window.

Transept – The cross-arm of a church. A wing which projects laterally from a church.

Zoomorphic – In animal form.